rainbow

in Cashsoft DK & Cashsoft Baby DK

pattern instruction page 70

🐦 *ashton*

in Cahner

pattern instruction page 40

patch blanket
in Cashsoft DK
pattern instruction page 83

griffen
in Handknit Cotton

pattern instruction page 50

summer

in Fine Milk Cotton

pattern instruction page 59

summer

in Fine Milk Cotton

pattern instruction page 59

trent
in Fine Milk Cotton
pattern instruction page 80

✑ *blossom*

in Fine Milk Cotton

pattern instruction page 44

floyd
in Handknit Cotton
pattern instruction page 48

sunny

in Fine Milk Cotton

pattern instruction page 76

sunny

in Fine Milk Cotton

pattern instruction page 76

jay
in Rowan Denim
pattern instruction page 54

quinn
in Rowan Denim
pattern instruction page 56

skye

in Handknit Cotton

pattern instruction page 74

starr

in Cashsoft DK

pattern instruction page 72

sunshine
in Calmer
pattern instruction page 78

31

sunshine

in Calmer

pattern instruction page 78

moonbeam

in Cashsoft Baby DK

pattern instruction page 64

prudence
in Fine Milk Cotton
pattern instruction page 66

rufus
in Fine Milk Cotton
pattern instruction page 61

 *prudence*
in Fine Milk Cotton
pattern instruction page 66

 *rufus*
in Fine Milk Cotton
pattern instruction page 61

floyd
in Handknit Cotton
pattern instruction page 48

gallery

4 *rainbow*
pattern instruction page 70

6 *ashton*
pattern instruction page 40

6 *ashton*
pattern instruction page 40

8 *basil bear*
pattern instruction page 42

8 *clover cow*
pattern instruction page 52

8 *christian lion*
pattern instruction page 46

9 *patch blanket*
pattern instruction page 83

10 *griffen*
pattern instruction page 50

12 *summer*
pattern instruction page 59

14 *trent*
pattern instruction page 80

16 *blossom*
pattern instruction page 44

18 *floyd*
pattern instruction page 48

20 *sunny*
pattern instruction page 76

23 *jay*
pattern instruction page 54

24 *quinn*
pattern instruction page 56

26 *skye*
pattern instruction page 74

28 *starr*
pattern instruction page 72

29 *starr*
pattern instruction page 72

30 *sunshine*
pattern instruction page 78

32
pattern instruction page 78

33 *moonbeam*
pattern instruction page 64

34 *prudence*
pattern instruction page 66

35 *rufus*
pattern instruction page 61

37 *floyd*
pattern instruction page 48

Designer: Martin Storey

main image page 6 & 7

YARN

To fit age

0-3	3-6	6-9	9-12	12-18			months
					2	3	years

Rowan Calmer

| 4 | 4 | 4 | 5 | 5 | 5 | 5 | x 50gm |

(photographed in Preen 501 and Spice 502)

NEEDLES

1 pair 4mm (no 8) (US 6) needles
1 pair 5mm (no 6) (US 8) needles

BUTTONS – 5 x BN1121 from Bedecked.
Please see information page for contact details.

TENSION

21 sts and 38 rows to 10 cm measured over g st using 5mm (US 8) needles.

BACK

Using 4mm (US 6) needles cast on 53 [55: 57: 59: 61: 63: 65] sts.
Work in g st for 4 rows, ending with RS facing for next row.
Change to 5mm (US 8) needles.
Cont in g st until back meas 15 [15.5: 16: 16.5: 17: 17.5: 18] cm, ending with RS facing for next row.

Shape armholes

Cast off 3 sts at beg of next 2 rows.
47 [49: 51: 53: 55: 57: 59] sts.
Dec 1 st at each end of next 3 rows.
41 [43: 45: 47: 49: 51: 53] sts.
Cont straight until armhole meas 11 [11.5: 12: 12.5: 13: 13.5: 14] cm, ending with RS facing for next row.

Shape shoulders and back neck

Next row (RS): Cast off 3 [4: 4: 4: 5: 5: 6] sts, K until there are 7 [7: 8: 8: 8: 9: 9] sts on right needle and turn, leaving rem sts on a holder.
Work each side of neck separately.
Cast off 3 sts at beg of next row.
Cast off rem 4 [4: 5: 5: 5: 6: 6] sts.
With RS facing, rejoin yarn to rem sts, cast off centre 21 [21: 21: 23: 23: 23: 23] sts onto a holder, K to end.
Complete to match first side, reversing shapings.

LEFT FRONT

Using 4mm (US 6) needles cast on 27 [28: 29: 30: 31: 32: 33] sts.
Work in g st for 4 rows, ending with RS facing for next row.
Change to 5mm (US 8) needles.
Cont in g st until left front matches back to beg of armhole shaping, ending with RS facing for next row.

Shape armholes

Cast off 3 sts at beg of next row. 24 [25: 26: 27: 28: 29: 30] sts.
Work 1 row.
Dec 1 st at armhole edge of next 3 rows.
21 [22: 23: 24: 25: 26: 27] sts.
Cont straight until 13 [15: 15: 15: 17: 17: 17] rows less have been worked than on back to beg of shoulder shaping, ending with **WS** facing for next row.

Shape neck

Cast off 8 [7: 7: 8: 7: 7: 7] sts at beg of next row.
13 [15: 16: 16: 18: 19: 20] sts.
Dec 1 st at neck edge of next 3 rows, then on foll 2 [3: 3: 3: 4: 4: 4] alt rows, then on foll 4th row. 7 [8: 9: 9: 10: 11: 12] sts.
Work 1 row, ending with RS facing for next row.

Shape shoulder

Cast off 3 [4: 4: 4: 5: 5: 6] sts at beg of next row.
Work 1 row.
Cast off rem 4 [4: 5: 5: 5: 6: 6] sts.

RIGHT FRONT

Work to match left front, reversing shapings.

SLEEVES

Using 4mm (US 6) needles cast on 27 [29: 29: 31: 33: 33: 33] sts.
Work in g st for 4 rows, ending with RS facing for next row.
Change to 5mm (US 8) needles.
Cont in g st, shaping sides by inc 1 st at each end of next and every foll alt [4th: 4th: 4th: 6th: 6th: 6th] row to 35 [45: 41: 37: 51: 45: 47] sts, then on every foll 4th [6th: 6th: 6th: 8th: 8th: 8th] row until there are 47 [49: 51: 53: 55: 57: 59] sts.
Cont straight until sleeve meas 12 [14.5: 17: 19: 21: 23.5: 26] cm, ending with RS facing for next row.

Shape top

Cast off 3 sts at beg of next 2 rows.

41 [43: 45: 47: 49: 51: 53] sts.
Dec 1 st at each end of next and foll 2 alt rows, then on foll row, ending with RS facing for next row.
Cast off rem 33 [35: 37: 39: 41: 43: 45] sts.

MAKING UP
Press as described on the information page.
Join both shoulder seams using back stitch, or mattress stitch if preferred.

Hood
With RS facing and using 5mm (US 8) needles, beg and ending at front opening edges, pick up and knit 21 [22: 22: 23: 24: 24: 24] sts up right side of neck, 27 [27: 27: 29: 29: 29: 29] sts from back, then 21 [22: 22: 23: 24: 24: 24] sts down left side of neck. 69 [71: 71: 75: 77: 77: 77] sts.
Work in g st for 5 rows, ending with RS facing for next row.
Place marker on centre st of last row.
Next row (RS): K to marked st, M1, K marked st, M1, K to end.
Rep last 6 rows 3 times more. 77 [79: 79: 83: 85: 85: 85] sts.
Cont straight until hood meas 21 [21: 22: 22: 23: 23: 23] cm from pick-up row, ending with RS facing for next row.
Next row (RS): K to within 2 sts of marked st, K2tog, K marked st, K2tog, K to end.
Next row: Knit.
Rep last 2 rows twice more, and then first of these 2 rows (the dec row) again, ending with **WS** facing for next row.
69 [71: 71: 75: 77: 77: 77] sts.
Next row (WS): K to within 1 st of marked st, K2tog, K to end. 68 [70: 70: 74: 76: 76: 76] sts.
Next row: K34 [35: 35: 37: 38: 38: 38] and turn.
Fold hood in half with **WS** facing and, using a third needle, join top seam by casting off both sets of sts tog (by taking

one st from first needle tog with corresponding st from second needle).

Button band
Using 4mm (US 6) needles cast on 6 sts.
Work in g st until band, when slightly stretched, fits up entire front opening edge (left front for a girl or right front for a boy) from cast-on edge to seam at top of hood, ending with RS facing for next row.
Cast off.
Slip stitch band in place. Mark positions for 5 buttons on this band – first button to come 3 cm up from cast-on edge, top button to come 3 cm below hood pick-up row and rem 3 buttons evenly spaced between.

Buttonhole band
Work to match button band, with the addition of 5 buttonholes worked to correspond with positions marked for buttons as folls:
Buttonhole row (RS): K2, cast off 2 sts (to make a buttonhole – cast on 2 sts over these cast-off sts on next row), K to end.
Slip stitch this band in place, joining cast-off ends of bands.

Pockets (make 2)
Using 5mm (US 8) needles cast on 11 [11: 11: 13: 13: 13: 13] sts.
Work in g st for 2 rows, ending with RS facing for next row.
Next row (RS): K2, M1, K to last 2 sts, M1, K2.
Next row: Knit.
Rep last 2 rows twice more. 17 [17: 17: 19: 19: 19: 19] sts.
Work a further 21 [21: 21: 25: 25: 25: 25] rows, ending with **WS** facing for next row.
Cast off knitwise (on **WS**).
See information page for finishing instructions, setting in sleeves using the shallow set-in method. Sew pockets onto fronts as in photograph.

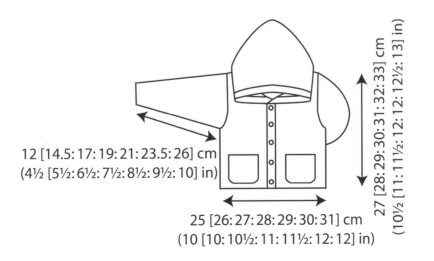

12 [14.5: 17: 19: 21: 23.5: 26] cm
(4½ [5½: 6½: 7½: 8½: 9½: 10] in)

27 [28: 29: 30: 31: 32: 33] cm
(10½ [11: 11½: 12: 12: 12½: 13] in)

25 [26: 27: 28: 29: 30: 31] cm
(10 [10: 10½: 11: 11½: 12: 12] in)

Designer: Martin Storey

main image page 8 & 9

YARN
Rowan Cashsoft DK

A Tape 515	3	x 50gm
B Blink 534	1	x 50gm
C Cream 500	1	x 50gm
D Thunder 518	1	x 50gm

NEEDLES
1 pair 3¼mm (no 10) (US 3) needles

EXTRAS
Washable toy filling. Shirring elastic.

TENSION
St st tension of 26 sts and 36 rows to 10 cm using 3¼mm (US 3) needles.

FINISHED SIZE
Completed toy stands approx 41 cm (16 ins) tall.

Bear
HEAD
Using 3¼mm (US 3) needles and yarn A cast on 16 sts.
Work in g st throughout as folls:
Inc 1 st at each end of 3rd and 3 foll 3rd rows. 24 sts.
Work 17 rows, ending with **WS** facing for next row.
Dec 1 st at each end of next and foll 3rd row, then on foll 4th row, then on 2 foll 3rd rows. 14 sts.
Inc 1 st at each end of next and 2 foll 3rd rows, then on foll 4th row, then on foll 3rd row. 24 sts.
Work 9 rows, ending with RS facing for next row.
Next row (RS): K17 and turn, leaving rem 7 sts on a holder.
Next row: K10 and turn, leaving rem 7 sts on a 2nd holder.
Work on this set of 10 sts only for top of nose.
Next row: sl 1, K9.
Rep last row 15 times more, ending with RS facing for next row.
Next row (RS): sl 1, K9, pick up and knit 8 sts down row-end edge of centre section, then K 7 sts from first holder.
Next row: K25, pick up and knit 8 sts down other row-end edge of centre section, then K 7 sts from 2nd holder. 40 sts.
Work 8 rows.
Shape chin
Row 1 (RS): (K2tog, K16, K2tog) twice. 36 sts.
Row 2: K16, (K2tog) twice, K16. 34 sts.
Row 3: K15 (K2tog) twice, K15. 32 sts.
Row 4: (K2tog, K12, K2tog) twice. 28 sts.
Row 5: K12, (K2tog) twice, K12. 26 sts.
Row 6: K11, (K2tog) twice, K11. 24 sts.
Row 7: (K2tog, K8, K2tog) twice. 20 sts.

Row 8: K8, (K2tog) twice, K8.
18 sts.
Row 9: K7, (K2tog) twice, K7.
Cast off rem 16 sts.
Fold head in half so that cast-on and cast-off edges match, then sew row-end edges together between fold and cast-on/cast-off edges. Insert toy filling, then join cast-on and cast-off edges.

BODY SECTIONS (make 2)
Using 3¼mm (US 3) needles and yarn A cast on 4 sts.
Work in g st throughout as folls:
Inc 1 st at each end of 2nd and foll 10 alt rows, then on 2 foll 6th rows. 30 sts.
Work 10 rows.
Dec 1 st at each end of next and 2 foll 6th rows, then on foll 5 alt rows. 14 sts.
Work 1 row, ending with RS facing for next row.
Cast off.
Join body sections along row-end and cast-on edges, leaving cast-off edges open. Insert toy filling. Attach head to cast-off edge of body sections, inserting a little more toy filling.

ARMS (make 2)
Using 3¼mm (US 3) needles and yarn A cast on 22 sts.
Work in g st throughout as folls:
Work 38 rows.
Shape hand
Row 1 (RS): (K2tog, K7, K2tog) twice. 18 sts.
Row 2: (K2tog, K5, K2tog) twice. 14 sts.
Row 3: (K2tog, K3, K2tog) twice. 10 sts.
Work 1 row, ending with RS facing for next row.
Cast off.
Fold arm in half lengthwise, then join row-end and cast-off edges, leaving cast-on edge open. Insert toy filling. Run gathering threads around cast-on edge, pull up tight and fasten off securely. Sew arms to body seams approx 3 cm (1¼ ins) down from head.

Using 3¼mm (US 3) needles and yarn A cast on 24 sts.
Work in g st throughout as folls:
Work 40 rows.
Shape ankle and foot
Row 1 (RS): (K1, K2tog) 8 times. 16 sts.
Work 1 row.
Row 3: K11 and turn, leaving rem 5 sts on a holder.
Row 4: K6 and turn, leaving rem 5 sts on a 2nd holder.
Work on this set of 6 sts only for top of foot.
Next row: sl 1, K5.
Rep last row 9 times more, ending with RS facing for next row.
Next row (RS): sl 1, K5, pick up and knit 6 sts down row-end edge of centre section, then K 5 sts from first holder.
Next row: K17, pick up and knit 6 sts down other row-end edge of centre section, then K 5 sts from 2nd holder. 28 sts.
Work 6 rows.
Shape sole
Row 1 (RS): (K2tog, K10, K2tog) twice. 24 sts.
Row 2: (K2tog, K8, K2tog) twice. 20 sts.
Row 3: (K2tog, K6, K2tog) twice. 16 sts.
Work 1 row, ending with RS facing for next row.
Cast off.
Fold leg in half lengthwise, then sew row-end and cast-off edges together. Insert toy filling. Run gathering threads around cast-on edge, pull up tight and fasten off securely. Sew legs to body seams at either end of cast-on edges of body sections.

Using 3¼mm (US 3) needles and yarn A cast on 8 sts.
Work in g st throughout as folls:
Inc 1 st at each end of 2nd and foll 4 rows. 18 sts.
Work 4 rows, ending with RS facing for next row.
Next row (RS): (K2tog) 9 times.
Cast off rem 9 sts.
Sew cast-off edges of ears to side seams of head, placing tops of ears level with end of seams.

Using photograph as a guide and yarn D, embroidery facial features as folls: For eyes, embroider chain stitch circle shapes. For nose, embroider a satin stitch triangle, then embroider chain stitch inverted "T" shape below for mouth.

Using 3¼mm (US 3) needles and yarn B cast on 53 sts.
Row 1 (RS): K1, ★P1, K1, rep from ★ to end.
Row 2: P1, ★K1, P1, rep from ★ to end.
These 2 rows form rib.
Work in rib for a further 4 rows, ending with RS facing for next row.
Join in yarn C and, beg with a K row, work in striped st st as folls:
Rows 1 and 2: Using yarn C.
Rows 3 and 4: Using yarn B.
These 4 rows form striped st st.
Cont in striped st st for a further 22 rows, ending with RS facing for next row.
Shape armholes
Keeping stripes correct, cast off 4 sts at beg of next 2 rows. 45 sts.
Dec 1 st at beg of next 4 rows. 41 sts.
Work 14 rows, ending with RS facing for next row.

Shape neck
Next row (RS): K9 and turn, leaving rem 32 sts on a holder.
Work a further 7 rows on these 9 sts only for first side of neck.
Cast off.
Return to sts on holder and slip centre 23 sts onto another holder. Rejoin appropriate yarn to rem 9 sts with RS facing and work 8 rows on these 9 sts for second side of neck.
Cast off.
Neckband
With RS facing, using 3¼mm (US 3) needles and yarn B, pick up and knit 6 sts down first side of neck, K across 23 sts left on holder, then pick up and knit 6 sts up other side of neck. 35 sts.
Work in rib as given for lower edge for 4 rows, ending with **WS** facing for next row.
Cast off in rib (on **WS**).

Using 3¼mm (US 3) needles and yarn B cast on 41 sts.
Work in rib as given for back and front for 6 rows, ending with RS facing for next row.
Join in yarn C.
Beg with 2 rows using yarn C, work in striped st st as given for back and front for 24 rows, ending with RS facing for next row.
Shape top
Keeping stripes correct, cast off 4 sts at beg of next 2 rows. 33 sts.
Dec 1 st at each end of next 8 rows. 17 sts.
Cast off 3 sts at beg of next 2 rows.
Cast off rem 11 sts.

Press as described on the information page.
Join shoulder and neckband seams. Sew sleeves into armholes, then join side and sleeve seams.

Using 3¼mm (US 3) needles and yarn B cast on 55 sts.
Row 1 (RS): K1, ★P1, K1, rep from ★ to end.
Row 2: P1, ★K1, P1, rep from ★ to end.
These 2 rows form rib.
Work in rib for a further 4 rows, ending with RS facing for next row.
Beg with a K row, cont in st st as folls:
Inc 1 st at each end of 7th and 3 foll 6th rows. 63 sts.
Work 5 rows, ending with RS facing for next row.
Shape leg openings
Cast off 4 sts at beg of next 14 rows. 7 sts.
Cast on 4 sts at beg of next 14 rows. 63 sts.
Dec 1 st at each end of 7th and 3 foll 6th rows. 55 sts.
Work 5 rows, ending with RS facing for next row.
Work in rib as given for cast-on edge for 6 rows, ending with RS facing for next row.
Cast off in rib.
Leg borders (both alike)
With RS facing, using 3¼mm (US 3) needles and yarn B, pick up and knit 49 sts all round cast-on and cast-off edges of leg openings.
Work in rib as given for cast-on edge for 3 rows, ending with RS facing for next row.
Cast off in rib.

Press as described on the information page.
Join side seams. Thread shirring elastic through waist ribbing, pulling up elastic to fit waist of bear.

blossom

Designer: Martin Storey

main image page 16 & 17

YARN

To fit age

0-3	3-6	6-9	9-12	12-18			
					2	3	years

Rowan Fine Milk Cotton

| 2 | 3 | 3 | 3 | 3 | 3 | 4 | x 50gm |

(photographed in Shrimps 483)

NEEDLES

1 pair 2mm (no 14) (US 0) needles
1 pair 2¾mm (no 12) (US 2) needles

BUTTONS

1 x BN1150 (small) from Bedecked.
Please see information page for contact details.

BEADS

5 small clear glass beads

TENSION

30 sts and 38 rows to 10 cm measured over st st using 2¾mm (US 2) needles.

BACK

Using 2¾mm (US 2) needles cast on 75 [79: 81: 85: 87: 91: 93] sts. Beg with a K row, work in st st for 22 [24: 24: 26: 28: 30: 32] rows, ending with RS facing for next row. (Back should meas 6 [6.5: 6.5: 7: 7.5: 8: 8.5] cm.)

Shape armholes

Cast off 3 [3: 3: 4: 4: 4: 4] sts at beg of next 2 rows.
69 [73: 75: 77: 79: 83: 85] sts.
Dec 1 st at each end of next 1 [1: 1: 3: 3: 3: 3] rows, then on foll 1 [2: 2: 1: 1: 2: 2] alt rows, then on foll 4th row.
63 [65: 67: 67: 69: 71: 73] sts.
Work 25 [25: 27: 29: 31: 31: 33] rows, ending with RS facing for next row. (Armhole should meas 9 [9.5: 10: 10.5: 11: 11.5: 12] cm.)

Shape shoulders and back neck

Next row (RS): Cast off 7 [7: 8: 7: 8: 8: 8] sts, K until there are 11 [11: 11: 11: 11: 11: 12] sts on right needle and turn, leaving rem sts on a holder.
Work each side of neck separately.
Cast off 3 sts at beg of next row.
Cast off rem 8 [8: 8: 8: 8: 8: 9] sts.
With RS facing, rejoin yarn to rem sts, cast off centre 27 [29: 29: 31: 31: 33: 33] sts, K to end.
Complete to match first side, reversing shapings.

LEFT FRONT

Using 2¾mm (US 2) needles cast on 10 [10: 11: 11: 11: 11: 11] sts. Beg with a K row, work in st st as folls:
Work 1 row, ending with **WS** facing for next row.
Cast on 10 [10: 11: 11: 11: 11: 11] sts at beg of next row.
20 [20: 22: 22: 22: 22: 22] sts.

Work 1 row.
Inc 1 st at beg of next row and at same edge of foll 9 [11: 9: 11: 11: 13: 13] rows, then on foll 4 [4: 5: 5: 6: 6: 7] alt rows.
34 [36: 37: 39: 40: 42: 43] sts.
Work 1 row, ending with RS facing for next row.

Shape armhole

Cast off 3 [3: 3: 4: 4: 4: 4] sts at beg and inc 1 st at end of next row. 32 [34: 35: 36: 37: 39: 40] sts.
Work 1 row.
Dec 1 st at armhole edge of next 1 [1: 1: 3: 3: 3: 3] rows and foll 1 [1: 1: 0: 0: 0: 0] alt rows **and at same time** inc 1 st at front opening edge of next and foll alt row.
32 [34: 35: 35: 36: 38: 39] sts.
Work 1 row, ending with RS facing for next row.

Shape front slope

Dec 1 st at end of next row and at same edge on foll 4 [4: 2: 2: 0: 0: 0] rows, then on foll 11 [12: 14: 15: 17: 18: 18] alt rows **and at same time** dec 1 st at armhole edge of 3rd [next: next: next: next: next: next] and foll 0 [0: 0: 0: 0: 1: 1] alt row, then on 0 [1: 1: 1: 1: 1: 1] foll 4th row. 15 [15: 16: 15: 16: 16: 17] sts.
Work 1 [1: 1: 1: 1: 1: 3] rows, ending with RS facing for next row.

Shape shoulder

Cast off 7 [7: 8: 7: 8: 8: 8] sts at beg of next row.
Work 1 row.
Cast off rem 8 [8: 8: 8: 8: 8: 9] sts.

RIGHT FRONT

Using 2¾mm (US 2) needles cast on 10 [10: 11: 11: 11: 11: 11] sts. Beg with a K row, work in st st as folls:
Work 2 rows, ending with RS facing for next row.
Cast on 10 [10: 11: 11: 11: 11: 11] sts at beg of next row.
20 [20: 22: 22: 22: 22: 22] sts.
Inc 1 st at end of next row and at same edge of foll 9 [11: 9: 11: 11: 13: 13] rows, then on foll 4 [4: 5: 5: 6: 6: 7] alt rows.

34 [36: 37: 39: 40: 42: 43] sts.
Complete to match left front, reversing shapings.

SLEEVES

Using 2¾mm (US 2) needles cast on 39 [43: 43: 45: 45: 49: 49] sts.
Beg with a K row, work in st st, shaping sides by inc 1 st at each end of 7th [13th: 13th: 9th: 9th: 13th: 13th] and every foll 8th [16th: 14th: 12th: 10th: 14th: 14th] row to 43 [49: 51: 55: 51: 53: 59] sts, then on every foll 10th [–: –: –: 12th: 16th: 16th] row until there are 47 [–: –: –: 57: 59: 61] sts.
Cont straight until sleeve meas 11.5 [14: 16.5: 18.5: 20.5: 23: 25.5] cm, ending with RS facing for next row.

Shape top
Cast off 3 [3: 3: 4: 4: 4: 4] sts at beg of next 2 rows.
41 [43: 45: 47: 49: 51: 53] sts.
Dec 1 st at each end of next 3 rows, then on foll alt row, then on 2 [3: 2: 3: 2: 3: 2] foll 4th rows. 29 [29: 33: 33: 37: 37: 41] sts.
Work 1 row, ending with RS facing for next row.
Dec 1 st at each end of next and foll 2 [1: 3: 2: 4: 3: 5] alt rows, then on foll row, ending with RS facing for next row.
Cast off rem 21 [23: 23: 25: 25: 27: 27] sts.

MAKING UP
Press as described on the information page.
Join both shoulder seams using back stitch, or mattress stitch if preferred. Join right side seam.

Body edging
Using 2mm (US 0) needles cast on 3 sts.
Row 1 (WS): P3.
Row 2: K1, yfwd, K1 tbl, P1. 4 sts.
Row 3: P2, (K1, P1, K1, P1) all into yfwd of previous row, P1. 7 sts.
Row 4: Cast off 4 sts (one st on right needle), K1 tbl, P1. 3 sts.
These 4 rows form patt.
Cont in patt until edging, beg and ending at base of left side seam, fits neatly around entire hem, front opening and neck edges, ending after patt row 4.
Cast off.
Slip stitch edging in place.

Cuff edgings (both alike)
Work as given for body edging, making a strip that fits neatly across sleeve cast-on edge.
Slip stitch edging in place.

See information page for finishing instructions, setting in sleeves using the set-in method.

Outer flower
Using 2mm (US 0) needles cast on 3 sts.
★★Row 1 (RS): K3.
Row 2 and every foll alt row: Purl.
Row 3: K1, (M1, K1) twice. 5 sts.
Row 5: K1, M1, K3, M1, K1. 7 sts.
Row 7: K1, M1, K5, M1, K1. 9 sts.
Row 9: K1, M1, K7, M1, K1. 11 sts.
Row 11: Knit.
Row 13: K2tog tbl, K7, K2tog. 9 sts.
Row 15: K2tog tbl, K5, K2tog. 7 sts.
Row 16: P2tog, P3, P2tog tbl. 5 sts.★★★
Break yarn and leave sts on needle – petal completed.
Onto same needle, cast on 3 sts.
Rep from ★★ 5 times more, then from ★★ to ★★★ again. 7 petals, 35 sts.
Next row (RS): (K2tog) 17 times, K1.
Break yarn and thread through rem 18 sts. Pull up tight and fasten off securely.

Inner flower
Using 2mm (US 0) needles cast on 3 sts.
★★Row 1 (RS): K3.
Row 2 and every foll alt row: Purl.
Row 3: K1, (M1, K1) twice. 5 sts.
Row 5: K1, M1, K3, M1, K1. 7 sts.
Row 7: K1, M1, K5, M1, K1. 9 sts.
Row 9: K2tog tbl, K5, K2tog. 7 sts.
Row 10: P2tog, P3, P2tog tbl. 5 sts.★★★
Break yarn and leave sts on needle – petal completed.
Onto same needle, cast on 3 sts.
Rep from ★★ 5 times more, then from ★★ to ★★★ again. 7 petals, 35 sts.
Next row (RS): (K2tog) 17 times, K1.
Break yarn and thread through rem 18 sts. Pull up tight and fasten off securely.
Using photograph as a guide, sew inner flower onto centre of outer flower, then attach to front at base of right front slope. Sew on beads at centre of inner flower. Attach button to left front at base of front slope, using one "loop" of edging as a buttonhole.

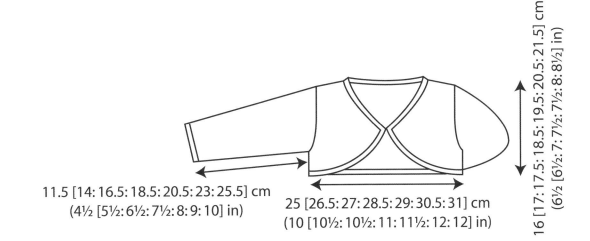

11.5 [14: 16.5: 18.5: 20.5: 23: 25.5] cm
(4½ [5½: 6½: 7½: 8: 9: 10] in)

25 [26.5: 27: 28.5: 29: 30.5: 31] cm
(10 [10½: 10½: 11: 11½: 12: 12] in)

16 [17: 17.5: 18.5: 19.5: 20.5: 21.5] cm
(6½ [6½: 7: 7½: 7½: 8: 8½] in)

Designer: Martin Storey

main image page 8 & 37

YARN

Rowan Fine Milk Cotton and Cashsoft 4 ply

A	Milk	Midget Gem 497	3	x 50gm
B	Cash	Bark 432	1	x 50gm

NEEDLES

1 pair 2¾mm (no 12) (US 2) needles
2.50mm (no 12) (US C2) crochet hook

EXTRAS

Washable toy filling. 2 buttons (for eyes).

TENSION

G st tension of 30 sts and 38 rows to 10 cm using 2¾mm
(US 2) needles.

FINISHED SIZE

Completed toy measures approx 31 cm (12 ins) from nose to tail
and stands approx 18 cm (7 ins) tall.

SPECIAL ABBREVIATIONS

loop 1 = insert right needle into next st as though to K this st,
wrap yarn over right needle point and first finger of left hand 3
times, then take yarn round right needle point as though to K
the st, draw all 4 loops through st on left needle and let st drop
from left needle. On next row, work each group of 4 loops tog
as one st.

CROCHET ABBREVIATIONS

ch = chain; **dc** = double crochet; **tr** = treble;
dtr = double treble.

SIDES (make 2)

Using 2¾mm (US 2) needles and yarn A cast on 18 sts.
Working in g st throughout, cont as folls:
Work 1 row, ending with **WS** facing for next row.
Inc 1 st at each end of next 3 rows, ending with RS facing for
next row. 24 sts.
Shape back leg
Cast on 16 sts at beg of next row. 40 sts.
★★Work 3 rows.
Next row (RS): K5 and turn.
Next row: sl 1, K4.
Work 2 rows across all sts.
Rep last 4 rows 3 times more, then first 2 of these rows again.★★
Cast off 18 sts at beg of next row. 22 sts.
Dec 1 st at beg of 2nd and foll 3 alt rows. 18 sts.

Work 5 rows, ending with RS facing for next row.
Inc 1 st at beg of next and 4 foll 6th rows, then on 2 foll 4th
rows **and at same time** dec 1 st at end of 14th row. 24 sts.
Work 8 rows, ending with **WS** facing for next row.
Inc 1 st at beg of next and foll 6 alt rows, ending with RS facing
for next row, **and at same time** inc 1 st at beg of 10th and foll
alt row. 33 sts.
Shape front leg
Cast on 14 sts at beg of next row. 47 sts.
Rep from ★★ to ★★ once more.
Cast off 16 sts at beg of next row. 31 sts.
Work 1 row, ending with RS facing for next row.
Dec 1 st at beg of next row and at same edge on foll 8 rows,
ending with **WS** facing for next row. 22 sts.
Place marker at beg of last row.
Dec 1 st at beg of next row and at same edge on 4 foll 3rd rows,
ending with RS facing for next row, **and at same time** inc 1 st
at beg of 6th and foll 2 alt rows. 20 sts.
Dec 1 st at beg of next 12 rows, ending with RS facing for
next row.
Cast off rem 8 sts.
Make a second side piece in exactly the same way but reading
RS for WS and vice versa.

UNDERBODY

Using 2¾mm (US 2) needles and yarn A cast on 2 sts.
Working in g st throughout, cont as folls:
Inc 1 st at each end of next and 3 foll 3rd rows. 10 sts.
Work 1 row, ending with **WS** facing for next row.
Shape back legs
Cast on 22 sts at beg of next 2 rows. 54 sts.
Next row (WS): K22, K2tog, (K2, K2tog) twice, K22. 51 sts.
Next row: K23, K2tog, K1, K2tog, K23. 49 sts.
★★**Next row:** K5 and turn.
Next row: sl 1, K4.

Work 1 row across all sts.
Rep last 3 rows 7 times more.★★
Next row (WS): K5 and turn.
Next row: sl 1, K4.
Cast off 18 sts at beg of next row.
Rep last 3 rows once more. 13 sts.
Dec 1 st at beg of next 7 rows. 6 sts.
Work 1 row, ending with **WS** facing for next row.
Inc 1 st at each end of next and foll alt row. 10 sts.
Work 46 rows, ending with RS facing for next row.
Inc 1 st at beg of next 4 rows. 14 sts.
Shape front legs
Cast on 14 sts at beg of next 2 rows. 42 sts.
Rep from ★★ to ★★ once more.
Next row (WS): K5 and turn.
Next row: sl 1, K4.
Cast off 16 sts at beg of next row.
Rep last 3 rows once more. 10 sts.
Dec 1 st at each end of next and foll 3 rows, ending with RS facing for next row.
Next row (RS): K2tog and fasten off.

MANE

Using 2¾mm (US 2) needles and yarn B cast on 30 sts.
Row 1 (RS): Knit.
Row 2: K1, ★loop 1, rep from ★ to last st, K1.
Rep last 2 rows once more, then row 1 again.
Row 6 (WS): K1, (loop 1) 23 times, K1 and turn.
Row 7: K20 and turn.
Row 8: As row 2.
Row 9: K to end.
Rep last 4 rows 3 times more.
Work 4 rows, ending with RS facing for next row.
Next row (RS): Cast off 9 sts, K to last 9 sts, cast off rem 9 sts.
Break yarn.
With **WS** facing, rejoin yarn to centre 12 sts and cont as folls:
Next row (WS): K1, (Loop 1) 10 times, K1.
Next row: Knit.

Rep last 2 rows once more, then first of these 2 rows again.
Cast off.

EARS (make 2)

Using 2.50mm (US C2) crochet hook and yarn A make 6 ch.
Row 1 (RS): 1 dc into 2nd ch from hook, 1 dc into each of next 4 ch, turn. 5 sts.
Row 2: 1 ch (does NOT count as st), 2 dc into first dc, (1 dc and 1 tr) into next dc, 1 dtr into next dc, (1 tr and 1 dc) into next dc, 2 dc into last dc, turn. 9 sts.
Row 3: 1 ch (does NOT count as st), 1 dc into each of first 2 dc, (1 dc and 1 tr) into next st, 2 tr into next st, 1 dtr into next st, 2 tr into next st, (1 tr and 1 dc) into next st, 1 dc into each of last 2 dc, turn. 13 sts.
Row 4: 1 ch (does NOT count as st), 1 dc into each of first 6 sts, 3 dc into next st, 1 dc into each of last 6 sts. 15 sts.
Fasten off.

MAKING UP
Do NOT press.
Matching fasten-off point of underbody to marker on sides, sew underbody to sides and legs. Join upper edges of sides between ends of underbody, leaving an opening to insert toy filling. Insert toy filling so toy is firmly filled and will stand on its own, then close opening. Using photograph as a guide, sew mane onto top of head, positioning cast-off edge of mane approx 5 cm (2 ins) back from cast-off edges at front of head. Shaping foundation ch edge of ears into a slight curve, sew ears to mane as in photograph. Using yarn B, embroidery a satin stitch nose and straight stitch mouth at front end of head. Attach buttons to form eyes. (**Note**: If giving toy to a very small child ensure button eyes are attached **very** securely. Alternatively, embroider eyes in satin stitch using yarn B.) Underneath chin, embroider a few loops using yarn A to form chin tuft. For tail, make a 10 cm (4 ins) long plait using 4 strands of yarn A for each strand of plait. Knot one end, enclosing a strand of yarn B, and trim ends to form a tassel approx 4 cm (1½ ins) long. Unravel strands of yarn within tassel. Attach other end of tail to back of lion as in photograph.

floyd

Designer: Martin Storey

main image page 18, 19 & 37

YARN

To fit age

0-3	3-6	6-9	9-12	12-18	2	3	
					2	3	years

Rowan Handknit Cotton

| 2 | 2 | 3 | 3 | 3 | 3 | 3 | x 50gm |

(photographed in Cloud 345 and Slate 347)

NEEDLES

1 pair 3¼mm (no 10) (US 3) needles
1 pair 4mm (no 8) (US 6) needles

BUTTONS

4 x BN1150 (small) from Bedecked.
Please see information page for details.

TENSION

20 sts and 28 rows to 10 cm measured over st st using 4mm (US 6) needles.

BACK

Using 3¼mm (US 3) needles cast on 48 [50: 52: 54: 56: 58: 60] sts.

Row 1 (RS): K3 [2: 3: 2: 3: 2: 3], *P2, K2, rep from * to last 1 [0: 1: 0: 1: 0: 1] st, K1 [0: 1: 0: 1: 0: 1].

Row 2: P3 [2: 3: 2: 3: 2: 3], *K2, P2, rep from * to last 1 [0: 1: 0: 1: 0: 1] st, P1 [0: 1: 0: 1: 0: 1].

These 2 rows form rib.

Work in rib for a further 4 rows, ending with RS facing for next row.

Change to 4mm (US 6) needles.

Beg with a K row, work in st st until back meas 14.5 [15.5: 16.5: 17.5: 18.5: 19.5: 20] cm, ending with RS facing for next row.

Shape armholes

Cast off 2 [2: 3: 3: 3: 3: 4] sts at beg of next 2 rows.

44 [46: 46: 48: 50: 52: 52] sts.★★

Dec 1 st at each end of next 3 rows, then on foll 1 [1: 1: 1: 2: 2: 2] alt rows, then on 0 [0: 1: 1: 1: 1: 1] foll 4th row.

36 [38: 36: 38: 38: 40: 40] sts.

Work 3 [3: 1: 3: 3: 3: 5] rows, ending with RS facing for next row.

Divide for back opening

Next row (RS): (K2tog) 1 [1: 0: 0: 0: 0: 0] times, K15 [16: 17: 18: 18: 19: 19] and turn, leaving rem sts on a holder.

16 [17: 17: 18: 18: 19: 19] sts.

Work each side of neck separately.

Work 19 rows, ending with RS facing for next row. (Armhole should meas 10.5 [10.5: 11.5: 12: 12: 13: 13.5] cm.)

Shape shoulder and back neck

Next row (RS): Cast off 2 [3: 3: 3: 3: 3: 3] sts, K until there are 6 sts on right needle and turn, leaving rem 8 [8: 8: 9: 9: 10: 10] sts

on a second holder.

Cast off 3 sts at beg of next row.

Cast off rem 3 sts.

With RS facing, rejoin yarn to rem sts on first holder, cast off centre 2 sts, K to last 2 [2: 0: 0: 0: 0: 0] sts, (K2tog) 1 [1: 0: 0: 0: 0: 0] times. 16 [17: 17: 18: 18: 19: 19] sts.

Complete to match first side, reversing shapings.

POCKET FLAP

Using 3¼mm (US 3) needles cast on 10 [11: 11: 12: 12: 13: 13] sts.

Work in g st for 2 rows, ending with RS facing for next row.

Row 3 (RS): Knit.

Row 4: K2, P to last 2 sts, K2.

Rep last 2 rows 3 [3: 3: 3: 4: 4: 4] times more, ending with RS facing for next row.

Break yarn and leave sts on a holder.

FRONT

Work as given for back to ★★.

Dec 1 st at each end of next 3 rows, then on foll 1 [1: 1: 1: 2: 2: 2] alt rows. 36 [38: 38: 40: 40: 42: 42] sts.

Work 1 [1: 1: 3: 1: 3: 3] rows, ending with RS facing for next row.

Place pocket flap

Next row (RS): (K2tog) 0 [0: 0: 1: 0: 1: 1] times, K2 [2: 2: 1: 2: 1: 1], holding WS of pocket flap against RS of front, K tog first st of flap with next st of front, (K tog next st of flap with next st of front) 9 [10: 10: 11: 11: 12: 12] times, K to last 0 [0: 0: 2: 0: 2: 2] sts, (K2tog) 0 [0: 0: 1: 0: 1: 1] times.

36 [38: 38: 38: 40: 40: 40] sts.

Dec 1 [1: 1: 0: 1: 0: 0] st at each end of 2nd row.

34 [36: 36: 38: 38: 40: 40] sts.

Cont straight until 12 rows less have been worked than on back to beg of shoulder shaping, ending with RS facing for next row.

Shape front neck

Next row (RS): K12 [13: 13: 13: 13: 13: 13] and turn, leaving rem sts on a holder.

Work each side of neck separately.

Dec 1 st at neck edge of next 4 rows, then on foll 3 alt rows.
5 [6: 6: 6: 6: 6: 6] sts.

Work 1 row, ending with RS facing for next row.

Shape shoulder

Cast off 2 [3: 3: 3: 3: 3: 3] sts at beg of next row.

Work 1 row.

Cast off rem 3 sts.

With RS facing, slip centre 10 [10: 10: 12: 12: 14: 14] sts onto a second holder, rejoin yarn to rem sts, K to end.

Complete to match first side, reversing shapings.

MAKING UP

Press as described on the information page.

Join both shoulder seams using back stitch, or mattress stitch if preferred.

Buttonhole border

With RS facing and using 3¼mm (US 3) needles, pick up and knit 15 sts evenly up left side of back opening, from cast-off sts at base of opening to sts left on holder at neck edge.

Work in g st for 1 row, ending with RS facing for next row.

Row 2 (RS): K3, (K2tog, yfwd, K4) twice.

Work in g st for a further 2 rows, ending with **WS** facing for next row.

Cast off knitwise (on **WS**).

Button border

With RS facing and using 3¼mm (US 3) needles, pick up and knit 15 sts evenly down right side of back opening, from sts left on holder at neck edge to cast-off sts at base of opening.

Work in g st for 4 rows, ending with **WS** facing for next row.

Cast off knitwise (on **WS**).

Lay buttonhole band over button band and sew row-end edges of bands to cast-off sts at base of opening.

Neckband

With RS facing and using 3¼mm (US 3) needles, pick up and knit 3 sts across top of buttonhole band, K8 [8: 8: 9: 9: 10: 10] sts on left back holder, pick up and knit 4 sts up left side of back neck and 14 sts down left side of front neck, K10 [10: 10: 12: 12: 14: 14] sts on front holder, pick up and knit 14 sts up right side of front neck and 4 sts down right side of back neck, K8 [8: 8: 9: 9: 10: 10] sts on right back holder, then pick up and knit 3 sts across top of button band.
68 [68: 68: 72: 72: 76: 76] sts.

Work in g st for 1 row, ending with RS facing for next row.

Row 2 (RS): K1, K2tog, yfwd, K to end.

Work in g st for a further 2 rows, ending with **WS** facing for next row.

Cast off knitwise (on **WS**).

Armhole borders (both alike)

With RS facing and using 3¼mm (US 3) needles, pick up and knit 46 [50: 54: 54: 58: 58: 62] sts evenly all round armhole edge.

Row 1 (WS): P2, ★K2, P2, rep from ★ to end.

Row 2: K2, ★P2, K2, rep from ★ to end.

Rep last 2 rows once more, ending with **WS** facing for next row.

Cast off in rib (on **WS**).

See information page for finishing instructions.

Pocket

Using 3¼mm (US 3) needles cast on 10 [11: 11: 12: 12: 13: 13] sts.

Work in g st for 2 rows, ending with RS facing for next row.

Row 3 (RS): Knit.

Row 4: K2, P to last 2 sts, K2.

Rep last 2 rows 8 [9: 9: 10: 11: 11: 12] times more, ending with RS facing for next row.

Cast off.

Using photograph as a guide, sew pocket onto front underneath pocket flap. Attach button to flap as in photograph.

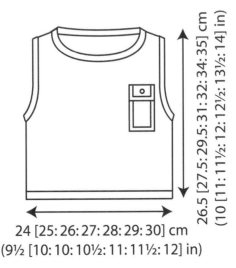

26.5 [27.5: 29.5: 31: 32: 34: 35] cm
(10 [11: 11½: 12: 12½: 13½: 14] in)

24 [25: 26: 27: 28: 29: 30] cm
(9½ [10: 10: 10½: 11: 11½: 12] in)

griffen

Designer: Martin Storey

main image page 10 & 11

YARN

To fit age

0-3	3-6	6-9	9-12	12-18			months
					2	3	years

Rowan Handknit Cotton

| 3 | 3 | 4 | 4 | 5 | 5 | 6 | x 50gm |

(photographed in Linen 205)

NEEDLES

1 pair 3¹/4mm (no 10) (US 3) needles
1 pair 4mm (no 8) (US 6) needles
3¹/4mm (no 10) (US 3) circular needle

TENSION

20 sts and 28 rows to 10 cm measured over st st using 4mm (US 6) needles.

BACK

Using 3¹/4mm (US 3) needles cast on 51 [53: 55: 57: 59: 61: 63] sts.
Row 1 (RS): K0 [0: 0: 0: 1: 2: 0], P0 [1: 2: 3: 3: 3: 0], ★K3, P3, rep from ★ to last 3 [4: 5: 0: 1: 2: 3] sts, K3 [3: 3: 0: 1: 2: 3], P0 [1: 2: 0: 0: 0: 0].
Row 2: P0 [0: 0: 0: 1: 2: 0], K0 [1: 2: 3: 3: 3: 0], ★P3, K3, rep from ★ to last 3 [4: 5: 0: 1: 2: 3] sts, P3 [3: 3: 0: 1: 2: 3], K0 [1: 2: 0: 0: 0: 0].
These 2 rows form rib.
Cont in rib for a further 12 rows, ending with RS facing for next row.
Change to 4mm (US 6) needles.
Beg and ending rows as indicated and repeating the 34 row patt rep throughout, now work in patt from chart as folls:
Cont straight until back meas 14 [15: 16: 17: 18: 19: 20] cm, ending with RS facing for next row.
Shape armholes
(**Note:** Armhole shaping is NOT shown on chart.)
Keeping patt correct, cast off 3 sts at beg of next 2 rows.
45 [47: 49: 51: 53: 55: 57] sts.
Dec 1 st at each end of next and foll 2 alt rows.
39 [41: 43: 45: 47: 49: 51] sts.
Cont straight until armhole meas 10.5 [11: 11.5: 12: 12.5: 13: 13.5] cm, ending with RS facing for next row.
Shape shoulders and back neck
Next row (RS): Cast off 3 [3: 4: 4: 5: 5: 5] sts, patt until there are 7 [7: 7: 8: 8: 8: 9] sts on right needle and turn, leaving rem sts on a holder.
Work each side of neck separately.
Cast off 3 sts at beg of next row.

Cast off rem 4 [4: 4: 5: 5: 5: 6] sts.
With RS facing, slip centre 19 [21: 21: 21: 21: 23: 23] sts onto a holder, rejoin yarn to rem sts, patt to end.
Complete to match first side, reversing shapings.

FRONT

Work as given for back until 8 [8: 8: 8: 10: 10: 10] rows less have been worked than on back to beg of shoulder shaping, ending with RS facing for next row.
Shape front neck
Next row (RS): Patt 12 [12: 13: 14: 16: 16: 17] sts and turn, leaving rem sts on a holder.
Work each side of neck separately.
Keeping patt correct, dec 1 st at neck edge of next 4 rows, then on foll 1 [1: 1: 1: 2: 2: 2] alt rows. 7 [7: 8: 9: 10: 10: 11] sts.
Work 1 row, ending with RS facing for next row.
Shape shoulder
Cast off 3 [3: 4: 4: 5: 5: 5] sts at beg of next row.
Work 1 row.
Cast off rem 4 [4: 4: 5: 5: 5: 6] sts.
With RS facing, slip centre 15 [17: 17: 17: 15: 17: 17] sts onto a holder, rejoin yarn to rem sts, patt to end.
Complete to match first side, reversing shapings.

SLEEVES

Using 3¹/4mm (US 3) needles cast on 27 [29: 29: 31: 31: 33: 33] sts.
Row 1 (RS): P0 [1: 1: 2: 2: 3: 3], ★K3, P3, rep from ★ to last 3 [4: 4: 5: 5: 0: 0] sts, K3 [3: 3: 3: 3: 0: 0], P0 [1: 1: 2: 2: 0: 0].
Row 2: K0 [1: 1: 2: 2: 3: 3], ★P3, K3, rep from ★ to last 3 [4: 4: 5: 5: 0: 0] sts, P3 [3: 3: 3: 3: 0: 0], K0 [1: 1: 2: 2: 0: 0].
These 2 rows form rib.
Cont in rib for a further 12 rows, ending with RS facing for next row.
Change to 4mm (US 6) needles.

Beg and ending rows as indicated, now work in patt from chart, shaping sides by inc 1 st at each end of next [next: next: next: next: 3rd: 3rd] and foll 2 [0: 0: 0: 0: 0: 0] rows, then on foll 5 [4: 3: 2: 1: 0: 0] alt rows, then on 0 [3: 5: 6: 8: 7: 7] foll 4th rows, then on 0 [0: 0: 0: 0: 2: 3] foll 6th rows, taking inc sts into patt. 43 [45: 47: 49: 51: 53: 55] sts.

Cont straight until sleeve meas 12 [14.5: 17: 19: 21: 23.5: 26] cm, ending with RS facing for next row.

Shape top

Keeping patt correct, cast off 3 sts at beg of next 2 rows. 37 [39: 41: 43: 45: 47: 49] sts.

Dec 1 st at each end of next and foll 2 alt rows, then on foll row, ending with RS facing for next row.

Cast off rem 29 [31: 33: 35: 37: 39: 41] sts.

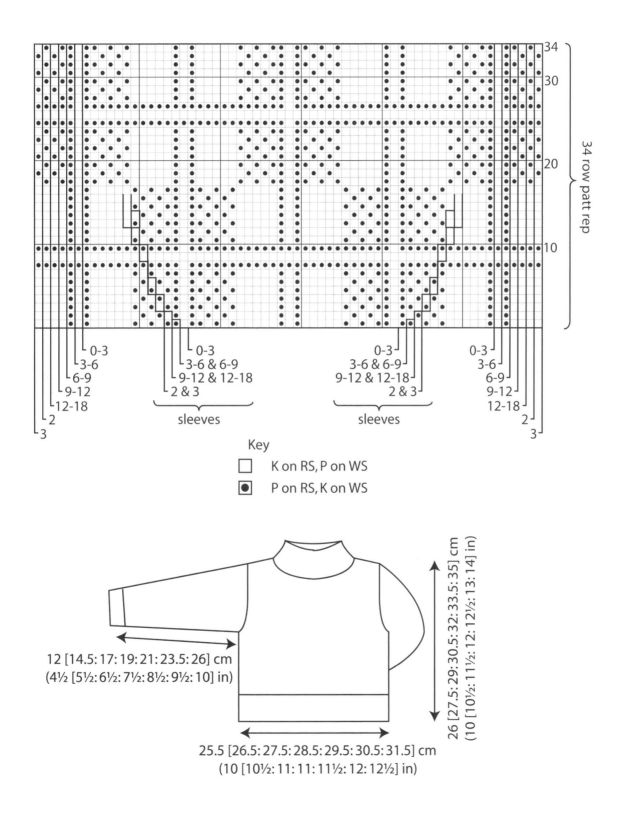

Key

☐   K on RS, P on WS

⦿   P on RS, K on WS

12 [14.5: 17: 19: 21: 23.5: 26] cm
(4½ [5½: 6½: 7½: 8½: 9½: 10] in)

26 [27.5: 29: 30.5: 32: 33.5: 35] cm
(10 [10½: 11½: 12: 12½: 13: 14] in)

25.5 [26.5: 27.5: 28.5: 29.5: 30.5: 31.5] cm
(10 [10½: 11: 11: 11½: 12: 12½] in)

Press as described on the information page.

Join both shoulder seams using back stitch, or mattress stitch if preferred.

Collar

With RS facing and using 3¼mm (US 3) circular needle, pick up and knit 9 [10: 10: 10: 11: 12: 12] sts down left side of front neck, K across 15 [17: 17: 17: 15: 17: 17] sts on front holder inc 1 st at centre, pick up and knit 9 [10: 10: 10: 11: 12: 12] sts up right side of front neck and 3 sts down right side of back neck, K across 19 [21: 21: 21: 21: 23: 23] sts on back holder inc 1 st at centre, then pick up and knit 3 sts up left side of back neck. 60 [66: 66: 66: 66: 72: 72] sts.

Round 1 (RS): ★K3, P3, rep from ★ to end.

Rep this round until collar meas 4 [4: 5: 5: 6: 6: 6] cm from pick-up round.

Next round: Knit.

Rep last round 5 times more.

Using a 4mm (US 6) needle, cast off **loosely** knitwise.

See information page for finishing instructions, setting in sleeves using the shallow set-in method.

clover cow

Designer: Martin Storey

main image page 8

YARN

A Cloud 497	3	x 50gm
B Slosh 479	1	x 50gm

NEEDLES

1 pair 3¼mm (no 10) (US 3) needles
1 pair 3¾mm (no 9) (US 5) needles
3.50mm (no 9) (US E4) crochet hook

EXTRAS

Washable toy filling. Oddments of yellow and green DK weight yarn for flowers and leaves.

TENSION

G st tension of 21 sts and 30 rows to 10 cm using 5mm (US 8) needles.

FINISHED SIZE

Completed toy measures approx 26 cm (10 ins) from nose to tail and stands approx 15 cm (6 ins) tall.

CROCHET ABBREVIATIONS

ch = chain; **dc** = double crochet; **tr** = treble; **dtr** = double treble; **ss** = slip stitch.

LEG (make 2)

Using 3¾mm (US 5) needles and yarn A cast on 40 sts.

Noting that first row is a **WS** row, work in g st throughout as folls:

Work 8 rows, ending with **WS** facing for next row.

★★Shape back leg

Cast off 24 sts at beg of next row. 16 sts.

Inc 1 st at end of next row, then at beg of foll row, ending with RS facing for next row. 18 sts.

Using the **intarsia** technique as described on the information page, join in yarn B and work patch as folls:

Row 1 (RS): Using yarn B K3, using yarn A K14, inc in last st.

Row 2: Using yarn A inc in first st, K15, using yarn B K3.

Row 3: Using yarn B K6, using yarn A K13, inc in last st.

Row 4: Using yarn A inc in first st, K14, using yarn B K6.

Row 5: Using yarn B K9, using yarn A K12, inc in last st.

Row 6: Using yarn A inc in first st, K13, using yarn B K9. 24 sts.

Row 7: Using yarn B K15, using yarn A K9.

Row 8: Using yarn A K9, using yarn B K15.

Rows 9 to 12: As rows 8 and 9, twice.

Row 13: Using yarn B K17, using yarn A K7.

Row 14: Using yarn A K7, using yarn B K17.

Row 15: Using yarn B K20, using yarn A K4.

Row 16: Using yarn A K4, using yarn B K20.

Rows 17 to 20: As rows 15 and 16, twice.

Row 21: Using yarn B K18, using yarn A K6.
Row 22: Using yarn A K6, using yarn B K18.
Row 23: Using yarn B K16, using yarn A K8.
Row 24: Using yarn A K8, using yarn B K16.
Row 25: Using yarn B K14, using yarn A K10.
Row 26: Using yarn A K10, using yarn B K14.
Row 27: Using yarn B K12, using yarn A K12.
Row 28: Using yarn A K12, using yarn B K12.
Row 29: Using yarn B K10, using yarn A K14.
Row 30: Using yarn A K14, using yarn B K10.
Rows 31 to 40: As rows 29 and 30, 5 times.
Row 41: Using yarn B K8, using yarn A K16.
Row 42: Using yarn A K16, using yarn B K8.
These 42 rows complete patch.
Break off yarn B and cont using yarn A **only**.
Dec 1 st at end of next and foll alt row, then at beg of foll alt row, ending with **WS** facing for next row. 21 sts.★★

Shape front leg
Cast on 16 sts at beg of next row. 37 sts.
Work 7 rows, ending with **WS** facing for next row.
Cast off 16 sts at beg of next row. 21 sts.
Dec 1 st at beg of next row. 20 sts.
Dec 1 st at beg of next and foll 7 alt rows. 12 sts.
Work 3 rows, placing marker at end of first of these rows and ending with **WS** facing for next row.
Inc 1 st at beg of next and foll alt row. 14 sts.
Work 6 rows, ending with RS facing for next row.

Shape horn
Cast on 6 sts at beg of next row. 20 sts.
Dec 1 st at end of next and foll alt row. 18 sts.
Cast off 4 sts at beg of next row. 14 sts.
Inc 1 st at beg of next row. 15 sts.
Work 1 row, ending with **WS** facing for next row.
Cast off.

RIGHT SIDE
Work to match left side, reversing all shaping and patch.

UNDERBODY
Using 3¾mm (US 5) needles and yarn A cast on 2 sts.
Noting that first row is a **WS** row, work in g st throughout as folls:
Inc 1 st at each end of next and foll alt row. 6 sts.
Work 3 rows, ending with **WS** facing for next row.

Shape back legs
Cast on 24 sts at beg of next 2 rows. 54 sts.
Next row (WS): K24, K2tog, K2, K2tog, K24. 52 sts.
Next row: K24, (K2tog) twice, K24. 50 sts.
Next row: K24, K2tog, K24. 49 sts.
Work 3 rows, ending with **WS** facing for next row.
Cast off 23 sts at beg of next 2 rows. 3 sts.

Shape udder
Inc 1 st at each end of next 3 rows. 9 sts.
Work 9 rows.
Dec 1 st at each end of next 2 rows. 5 sts.
Inc 1 st at each end of next 2 rows. 9 sts.
Work 9 rows.
Dec 1 st at each end of next 2 rows. 5 sts.
Udder section is now complete.
Work 30 rows, ending with **WS** facing for next row.

Shape front legs
Cast on 16 sts at beg of next 2 rows. 37 sts.
Work 6 rows.
Cast off 16 sts at beg of next 2 rows. 5 sts.
Work 7 rows, ending with RS facing for next row.
Dec 1 st at each end of next row. 3 sts.
Work 4 rows, ending with **WS** facing for next row.
Next row (WS): K2tog, K1.
Next row: K2tog and fasten off.

TOP OF HEAD
Using 3¾mm (US 5) needles and yarn A cast on 2 sts.
Noting that first row is a **WS** row, work in g st throughout as folls:
Row 1 (WS): Inc once in each st. 4 sts.
Work 9 rows, ending with **WS** facing for next row.

Shape horns
Cast on 6 sts at beg of next 2 rows. 16 sts.
Dec 1 st at beg of next 4 rows. 12 sts.
Cast off 4 sts at beg of next 2 rows. 4 sts.
Inc 1 st at each end of next row. 6 sts.
Work 5 rows, ending with **WS** facing for next row.
Dec 1 st at each end of next row. 4 sts.
Work 10 rows.
Next row (RS): Inc once in each st to end. 8 sts.
Work 4 rows, ending with **WS** facing for next row.
Cast off.

EARS (make 2)
Using 3.50mm (US E4) crochet hook and yarn A make 4 ch and join with a ss to form a ring.
Round 1 (RS): (6 dc, 3 tr and 1 dtr) into ring. 10 sts.
Fasten off.

MAKING UP
Do NOT press.
Form udder section on underbody by folding udder section in half and joining row-end edges to form a rounded bag shape. Matching fasten-off point of underbody to marker on sides, sew underbody to sides and legs. Join row-end edges of chin section of sides from marker to cast-off edge. Matching horn sections and centre of cast-off edge to top of joined chin seam, sew top of head to sides. Join rem edges of sides, leaving an opening to insert toy filling. Insert toy filling so toy is firmly filled and will stand on its own, ensuring filling is inserted into udder and horns, then close opening. Using photograph as a guide, sew ears onto head section near horns. Using yarn B, embroidery small circle shapes to form eyes and straight stitch nostrils. For tail, make a 9 cm (3½ ins) long plait using 3 strands of yarn B for each strand of plait. Knot one end, and trim ends to form a tassel approx 3 cm (1 in) long. Attach other end of tail to back of lion as in photograph.

Flowers (make 4)
Using 3¼mm (US 3) needles and oddment of yellow yarn, cast on 10 sts.
Knit 1 row.
Break yarn and thread through all 10 sts. Pull up tight and fasten off securely, joining row-end edges at same time.
Using oddment of green yarn, embroider loops along mouth edge, attaching flowers to loops.

Designer: Martin Storey

main image page 23

YARN

To fit age

0-3	3-6	6-9	9-12	12-18			
					2	3	years

months

Rowan Denim

| 4 | 4 | 5 | 5 | 6 | 6 | 6 | x 50gm |

(photographed in Tennessee 231)

NEEDLES

1 pair 3¼mm (no 10) (US 3) needles
1 pair 4mm (no 8) (US 6) needles
2 double-pointed 3¼mm (no 10) (US 3) needles

BUTTONS

5 x RW5022 from Bedecked.
Please see information page for contact details.

TENSION

Before washing: 20 sts and 28 rows to 10 cm measured over st st using 4mm (US 6) needles.

Tension note: Denim will shrink in length when washed for the first time. Allowances have been made in the pattern for shrinkage (see size diagram for after washing measurements).

BACK

Using 3¼mm (US 3) needles cast on 51 [53: 55: 57: 59: 61: 63] sts.
Beg with a K row, work in st st for 6 rows, ending with RS facing for next row.
Row 7 (RS): Purl (to form fold line).
Beg with a P row, work in st st for 5 rows, ending with RS facing for next row.
Change to 4mm (US 6) needles.
Cont in st st until back meas 15.5 [16.5: 17.5: 19: 20: 21: 22.5] cm
from fold line row, ending with RS facing for next row.
Shape armholes
Cast off 3 sts at beg of next 2 rows.
45 [47: 49: 51: 53: 55: 57] sts.
Dec 1 st at each end of next and foll 2 alt rows.
39 [41: 43: 45: 47: 49: 51] sts.
Cont straight until armhole meas 12.5 [13: 13.5: 14.5: 15: 15.5: 16] cm, ending with RS facing for next row.
Shape shoulders and back neck
Next row (RS): Cast off 3 [4: 4: 4: 5: 5: 6] sts, K until there are 7 [7: 8: 8: 8: 9: 9] sts on right needle and turn, leaving rem sts on a holder.
Work each side of neck separately.
Cast off 3 sts at beg of next row.
Cast off rem 4 [4: 5: 5: 5: 6: 6] sts.
With RS facing, rejoin yarn to rem sts, cast off centre 19 [19: 19: 21: 21: 21: 21] sts, K to end.
Complete to match first side, reversing shapings.

POCKET FLAP

Using 3¼mm (US 3) needles cast on 33 [37: 39: 43: 45: 49: 49] sts.
Work in g st for 3 rows, ending with **WS** facing for next row.
Row 4 (WS): Cast off 9 [11: 11: 13: 13: 15: 15] sts knitwise, P until there are 15 [15: 17: 17: 19: 19: 19] sts on right needle, cast off rem 9 [11: 11: 13: 13: 15: 15] sts knitwise.
Break yarn.
With RS facing and using 4mm (US 6) needles, rejoin yarn to centre 15 [15: 17: 17: 19: 19: 19] sts and K to end.
Beg with a P row, work in st st, inc 1 st at each end of next 4 rows. 23 [23: 25: 25: 27: 27: 27] sts.
Work a further 9 [11: 11: 13: 13: 15: 15] rows, ending with RS facing for next row.
Break yarn and leave sts on a holder.

FRONT

Using 3¼mm (US 3) needles cast on 51 [53: 55: 57: 59: 61: 63] sts.
Beg with a K row, work in st st for 6 rows, ending with RS facing for next row.
Row 7 (RS): Purl (to form fold line).
Row 8: Purl.
Row 9 (eyelet row): K22 [23: 24: 25: 26: 27: 28], K2tog, yfwd, K3, yfwd, sl 1, K1, psso, K to end.
Beg with a P row, work in st st for 3 rows, ending with RS facing for next row.
Change to 4mm (US 6) needles.
Cont in st st until 2 rows less have been worked than on back to beg of armhole shaping, ending with RS facing for next row.
Attach pocket flap
Next row (RS): K14 [15: 15: 16: 16: 17: 18], holding **WS** of pocket flap against RS of front K tog first st of pocket flap with next st of front, (K tog next st of pocket flap with next st of front) 22 [22: 24: 24: 26: 26: 26] times, K14 [15: 15: 16: 16: 17: 18].
Next row: Purl.

Shape armholes

Cast off 3 sts at beg of next 2 rows. 45 [47: 49: 51: 53: 55: 57] sts.

Dec 1 st at each end of next and foll 2 alt rows. 39 [41: 43: 45: 47: 49: 51] sts.

Work 1 row, ending with RS facing for next row.

Divide for front opening

Next row (RS): K17 [18: 19: 20: 21: 22: 23] and turn, leaving rem sts on a holder.

Work each side of neck separately.

Cont straight until 11 [11: 11: 11: 13: 13: 13] rows less have been worked than on back to beg of shoulder shaping, ending with **WS** facing for next row.

Shape neck

Cast off 5 [5: 5: 6: 5: 5: 5] sts at beg of next row.

12 [13: 14: 14: 16: 17: 18] sts.

Dec 1 st at neck edge of next 3 rows, then on foll 1 [1: 1: 1: 2: 2: 2] alt rows, then on foll 4th row. 7 [8: 9: 9: 10: 11: 12] sts.

Work 1 row, ending with RS facing for next row.

Shape shoulder

Cast off 3 [4: 4: 4: 5: 5: 6] sts at beg of next row.

Work 1 row.

Cast off rem 4 [4: 5: 5: 5: 6: 6] sts.

With RS facing, slip centre 5 sts onto a holder, rejoin yarn to rem sts, K to end.

Complete to match first side, reversing shapings.

SLEEVES

Using 3¼mm (US 3) needles cast on 26 [28: 28: 30: 30: 32: 32] sts.

Row 1 (RS): K2 [1: 1: 2: 2: 1: 1], *P2, K2, rep from * to last 0 [3: 3: 0: 0: 3: 3] sts, (P2, K1) 0 [1: 1: 0: 0: 1: 1] times.

Row 2: P2 [1: 1: 2: 2: 1: 1], *K2, P2, rep from * to last 0 [3: 3: 0: 0: 3: 3] sts, (K2, P1) 0 [1: 1: 0: 0: 1: 1] times.

These 2 rows form rib.

Work in rib for a further 10 [10: 12: 12: 14: 14: 14] rows, ending with RS facing for next row.

Change to 4mm (US 6) needles.

Beg with a K row, work in st st, shaping sides by inc 1 st at each end of next [next: next: 3rd: 3rd: 3rd: 3rd] and every foll alt [alt: 4th: 4th: 4th: 4th: 4th] row to 38 [32: 46: 46: 48: 42: 40] sts, then on every foll 4th [4th: –: 6th: 6th: 6th: 6th] row until there are 42 [44: –: 48: 50: 52: 54] sts.

Cont straight until sleeve meas 13.5 [16.5: 19.5: 21.5: 24: 27: 29.5] cm, ending with RS facing for next row.

Shape top

Cast off 3 sts at beg of next 2 rows. 36 [38: 40: 42: 44: 46: 48] sts.

Dec 1 st at each end of 2nd and foll 3rd row, then on foll alt row, then on foll row, ending with RS facing for next row.

Cast off rem 28 [30: 32: 34: 36: 38: 40] sts.

MAKING UP

Do NOT press.

Join both shoulder seams using back stitch, or mattress stitch if preferred.

Hood

With RS facing and using 4mm (US 6) needles, beg and ending at front opening edges, pick up and knit 20 [20: 20: 21: 22: 22: 22] sts up right side of neck, 27 [27: 27: 29: 29: 29: 29] sts from back, then 20 [20: 20: 21: 22: 22: 22] sts down left side of neck. 67 [67: 67: 71: 73: 73: 73] sts.

Beg with a P row, work in st st for 3 rows, ending with RS facing for next row.

Place marker on centre st of last row.

Next row (RS): K to marked st, M1, K marked st, M1, K to end.

Rep last 4 rows 3 times more. 75 [75: 75: 79: 81: 81: 81] sts.

Cont straight until hood meas 23 [23: 24: 24: 25: 25: 25] cm from pick-up row, ending with RS facing for next row.

Next row (RS): K to within 2 sts of marked st, K2tog tbl, K marked st, K2tog, K to end.

Next row: Purl.

Rep last 2 rows once more, and then first of these 2 rows (the dec row) again, ending with **WS** facing for next row. 69 [69: 69: 73: 75: 75: 75] sts.

Next row (WS): P to within 1 st of marked st, P2tog, P to end. 68 [68: 68: 72: 74: 74: 74] sts.

Next row: K34 [34: 34: 36: 37: 37: 37] and turn.

Fold hood in half with **WS** facing and, using a third needle, join top seam by casting off both sets of sts tog (by taking one st from first needle tog with corresponding st from second needle).

Button band

Using 3¼mm (US 3) needles cast on 5 sts.

Work in g st until band, when slightly stretched, fits up entire front opening edge (left front for a girl or right front for a boy) from sts at base of front opening to seam at top of hood, ending with RS facing for next row.

Cast off.

Slip stitch band in place. Mark positions for 3 buttons on this band – first button to come 1.5 cm up from base of front opening, top button to come level with hood pick-up row and rem button evenly spaced between.

Buttonhole band

Slip 5 sts from holder at base of front opening onto 3¼mm (US 3) needles and rejoin yarn with RS facing.

Complete to match button band, with the addition of 3 buttonholes worked to correspond with positions marked for buttons as folls:

Buttonhole row (RS): K1, K2tog, yfwd (to make a buttonhole), K2.

Slip stitch this band in place, joining cast-off ends of bands. Slip stitch cast-on edge of button band in place behind buttonhole band at base of opening.

Pocket

Using 3¼mm (US 3) needles cast on 27 [27: 29: 29: 31: 31: 31] sts.

Work in g st for 4 rows, ending with RS facing for next row.

Change to 4mm (US 6) needles.

Next row (RS): Knit.

Next row: K2, P to last 2 sts, K2.

Rep last 2 rows until pocket meas 8.5 [9.5: 10.5: 12: 13: 14: 15.5] cm, ending with RS facing for next row.

Change to 3¼mm (US 3) needles.

Work in g st for 5 rows, ending with **WS** facing for next row.

Cast off knitwise (on **WS**).

Cord

Using double-pointed 3¼mm (US 3) needles cast on 3 sts.

Row 1 (RS): K3, *without turning slip these 3 sts to opposite end of needle and bring yarn to opposite end of work pulling it quite tightly across **WS** of work, K these 3 sts again, rep from * until cord is 75 [75: 80: 80: 80: 85: 85] cm long.

Cast off.

Machine wash all pieces before completing sewing together.

See information page for finishing instructions, setting in sleeves using the shallow set-in method. Sew pocket onto front as in photograph, attaching 2 buttons to pocket flap. Around lower edge of body, fold first 6 rows to inside along fold line row and stitch in place to form casing. Thread cord through eyelets of casing and tie ends at centre front.

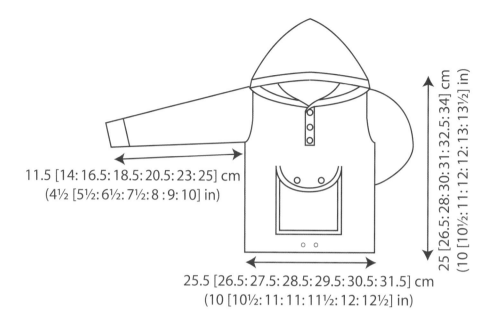

11.5 [14: 16.5: 18.5: 20.5: 23: 25] cm
(4½ [5½: 6½: 7½: 8 : 9: 10] in)

25 [26.5: 28: 30: 31: 32.5: 34] cm
(10 [10½: 11: 12: 12: 13: 13½] in)

25.5 [26.5: 27.5: 28.5: 29.5: 30.5: 31.5] cm
(10 [10½: 11: 11: 11½: 12: 12½] in)

quinn

Designer: Martin Storey

main image page 24 & 25

YARN

To fit age								
0-3	3-6	6-9	9-12	12-18			months
					2	3	years

4	4	5	5	5	6	6	x 50gm
(photographed in Memphis 229)

NEEDLES

1 pair 3¼mm (no 10) (US 3) needles
1 pair 4mm (no 8) (US 6) needles

BUTTONS

5 x BN1116 from Bedecked.
Please see information page for contact details.

TENSION

Before washing: 20 sts and 28 rows to 10 cm measured over st st using 4mm (US 6) needles.

Tension note: Denim will shrink in length when washed for the first time. Allowances have been made in the pattern for shrinkage (see size diagram for after washing measurements).

BACK

Using 3¼mm (US 3) needles cast on 50 [52: 54: 56: 58: 60: 62] sts.

Row 1 (RS): K0 [0: 0: 1: 0: 0: 0], P0 [1: 2: 2: 0: 1: 2], *K2, P2, rep from * to last 2 [3: 0: 1: 2: 3: 0] sts, K2 [2: 0: 1: 2: 2: 0], P0 [1: 0: 0: 0: 1: 0].
Row 2: P0 [0: 0: 1: 0: 0: 0], K0 [1: 2: 2: 0: 1: 2], *P2, K2, rep from * to last 2 [3: 0: 1: 2: 3: 0] sts, P2 [2: 0: 1: 2: 2: 0], K0 [1: 0: 0: 0: 1: 0].
These 2 rows form rib.
Cont in rib for a further 10 [10: 12: 12: 14: 14: 14] rows, ending with RS facing for next row.
Change to 4mm (US 6) needles.
Beg with a K row, work in st st until back meas 16 [16.5: 17.5: 19: 20: 21: 21.5] cm, ending with RS facing for next row.
Shape raglan armholes
Cast off 2 sts at beg of next 2 rows. 46 [48: 50: 52: 54: 56: 58] sts.
Next row (RS): K2, sl 1, K1, psso, K to last 4 sts, K2tog, K2.
Next row: K2, P to last 2 sts, K2.
Next row: Knit.
Next row: K2, P to last 2 sts, K2.
Rep last 4 rows 0 [1: 1: 2: 2: 3: 3] times more.
44 [44: 46: 46: 48: 48: 50] sts.
Next row (RS): K2, sl 1, K1, psso, K to last 4 sts, K2tog, K2.
Next row: K2, P to last 2 sts, K2.
Rep last 2 rows 13 [12: 13: 12: 13: 12: 13] times more, ending with RS facing for next row.
Cast off rem 16 [18: 18: 20: 20: 22: 22] sts.

Using 4mm (US 6) needles cast on 14 [16: 16: 18: 18: 20: 20] sts.
Beg with a K row, work in st st for 16 [16: 18: 18: 20: 20: 22] rows, ending with RS facing for next row.
Break yarn and leave sts on a holder.

Using 3¼mm (US 3) needles cast on 25 [26: 27: 28: 29: 30: 31] sts.
Row 1 (RS): K0 [0: 0: 1: 0: 0: 0], P0 [1: 2: 2: 0: 1: 2], *K2, P2, rep from * to last st, K1.
Row 2: P1, K2, *P2, K2, rep from * to last 2 [3: 0: 1: 2: 3: 0] sts, P2 [2: 0: 1: 2: 2: 0], K0 [1: 0: 0: 0: 1: 0].
These 2 rows form rib.
Cont in rib for a further 10 [10: 12: 12: 14: 14: 14] rows, ending with RS facing for next row.
Change to 4mm (US 6) needles.
Beg with a K row, work in st st for 16 [16: 18: 18: 20: 20: 22] rows, ending with RS facing for next row.
Place pocket
Next row (RS): K6 [5: 6: 5: 6: 5: 6], slip next 14 [16: 16: 18: 18: 20: 20] sts onto a holder and, in their place, K across 14 [16: 16: 18: 18: 20: 20] sts of first pocket lining, K5.
Cont in st st until left front matches back to beg of raglan armhole shaping, ending with RS facing for next row.
Shape raglan armhole
Cast off 2 sts at beg of next row. 23 [24: 25: 26: 27: 28: 29] sts.
Work 1 row.
Working all raglan armhole decreases in same way as given for back raglan armholes, dec 1 st at raglan armhole edge of next and 1 [2: 2: 3: 3: 4: 4] foll 4th rows, then on foll 7 [5: 6: 5: 5: 4: 5] alt rows, ending with **WS** facing for next row.
14 [16: 16: 17: 18: 19: 19] sts.
Shape neck
Cast off 5 [5: 5: 6: 5: 6: 6] sts at beg of next row. 9 [11: 11: 11:

13: 13: 13] sts.
Dec 1 st at neck edge of next 3 rows, then on foll 0 [1: 1: 1: 2: 2: 2] alt rows **and at same time** dec 1 st at raglan armhole edge of next and foll 1 [2: 2: 2: 3: 3: 3] alt rows. 4 sts.
Next row (WS): P2, K2.
Next row: K1, sl 1, K2tog, psso.
Next row: K2.
Next row: K2tog and fasten off.

Using 3¼mm (US 3) needles cast on 25 [26: 27: 28: 29: 30: 31] sts.
Row 1 (RS): K1, P2, *K2, P2, rep from * to last 2 [3: 0: 1: 2: 3: 0] sts, K2 [2: 0: 1: 2: 2: 0], P0 [1: 0: 0: 0: 1: 0].
Row 2: P0 [0: 0: 1: 0: 0: 0], K0 [1: 2: 2: 0: 1: 2], *P2, K2, rep from * to last st, P1.
These 2 rows form rib.
Cont in rib for a further 10 [10: 12: 12: 14: 14: 14] rows, ending with RS facing for next row.
Change to 4mm (US 6) needles.
Beg with a K row, work in st st for 16 [16: 18: 18: 20: 20: 22] rows, ending with RS facing for next row.
Place pocket
Next row (RS): K5, slip next 14 [16: 16: 18: 18: 20: 20] sts onto a holder and, in their place, K across 14 [16: 16: 18: 18: 20: 20] sts of second pocket lining, K6 [5: 6: 5: 6: 5: 6].
Complete to match left front, reversing shapings.

Using 3¼mm (US 3) needles cast on 26 [28: 28: 30: 30: 32: 32] sts.
Row 1 (RS): P2 [1: 1: 2: 2: 1: 1], *K2, P2, rep from * to last 0 [3: 3: 0: 0: 3: 3] sts, (K2, P1) 0 [1: 1: 0: 0: 1: 1] times.
Row 2: K2 [1: 1: 2: 2: 1: 1], *P2, K2, rep from * to last 0 [3: 3: 0: 0: 3: 3] sts, (P2, K1) 0 [1: 1: 0: 0: 1: 1] times.
These 2 rows form rib.
Work in rib for a further 10 [10: 12: 12: 14: 14: 14] rows, ending with RS facing for next row.
Change to 4mm (US 6) needles.
Beg with a K row, work in st st, shaping sides by inc 1 st at each end of next [next: next: next: next: 3rd: 3rd] and every foll alt [alt: alt: alt: alt: 4th: 4th] row to 44 [38: 36: 34: 34: 50: 48] sts, then on every foll - [4th: 4th: 4th: 4th: 6th: 6th] row until there are - [46: 48: 50: 52: 54: 56] sts.
Cont straight until sleeve meas 13 [16: 19: 21: 23.5: 26.5: 29] cm, ending with RS facing for next row.
Shape raglan
Cast off 2 sts at beg of next 2 rows.
40 [42: 44: 46: 48: 50: 52] sts.
Working all raglan decreases in same way as given for back raglan armholes, dec 1 st at each end of next and 3 foll 4th rows, then on every foll alt row until 20 sts rem.
Work 1 row, ending with RS facing for next row.
Left sleeve only
Dec 1 st at each end of next row, then cast off 4 sts at beg of foll row. 14 sts.
Dec 1 st at beg of next row, then cast off 4 sts at beg of foll row. 9 sts.
Right sleeve only
Cast off 5 sts at beg and dec 1 st at end of next row. 14 sts.
Work 1 row.
Cast off 4 sts at beg and dec 1 st at end of next row. 9 sts.

Work 1 row.
Both sleeves
Rep last 2 rows once more, ending with RS facing for next row.
Cast off rem 4 sts.

MAKING UP

Do NOT press.
Join all raglan seams using back stitch, or mattress stitch if preferred.
Button band
Using 3¼mm (US 3) needles cast on 7 sts.
Work in g st until band, when slightly stretched, fits up front opening edge (left front for a girl or right front for a boy) from cast-on edge to neck shaping, ending with RS facing for next row.
Cast off.
Slip stitch band in place. Mark positions for 5 buttons on this band – first button to come 3 cm up from cast-on edge, top button to come 3 cm below neck shaping and rem 3 buttons evenly spaced between.
Buttonhole band
Work to match button band, with the addition of 5 buttonholes worked to correspond with positions marked for buttons as folls:
Buttonhole row (RS): K3, cast off 2 sts (to make a buttonhole – cast on 2 sts over these cast-off sts on next row), K to end.
Slip stitch this band in place.
Collar
Using 3¼mm (US 3) needles cast on 7 sts.

Row 1 (RS): Knit.
Row 2: K1, inc in next st, K to last 3 sts, inc in next st, K2.
Rep last 2 rows 4 times more. 17 sts.
Row 11: Knit.
Row 12: K1, inc in next st, K to end.
Rep last 2 rows 7 times more. 25 sts.
Place marker at beg of last row.
Cont in g st until collar, unstretched, fits from top of front band, around neck edge and across to centre back neck, ending with RS facing for next row.
Place second marker at beg of last row.
Cont straight until work meas same from second marker as between first and second markers, ending with **WS** facing for next row.
Next row (WS): K1, K2tog, K to end.
Next row: Knit.
Rep last 2 rows 7 times more. 17 sts.
Next row (RS): K1, K2tog, K to last 3 sts, K2tog, K1.
Next row: Knit.
Rep last 2 rows 4 times more. 7 sts.
Cast off.
Pocket tops (both alike)
Slip 14 [16: 16: 18: 18: 20: 20] sts from pocket holder onto 3¼mm (US 3) needles and rejoin yarn with RS facing.
Work in g st for 5 rows, ending with **WS** facing for next row.
Cast off knitwise (on **WS**).
Machine wash all pieces before completing sewing together.
See information page for finishing instructions. Sew marked edge of collar to neck edge, matching cast-on and cast-off edges to top of front bands.

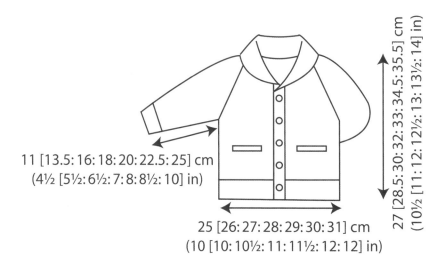

11 [13.5: 16: 18: 20: 22.5: 25] cm
(4½ [5½: 6½: 7: 8: 8½: 10] in)

25 [26: 27: 28: 29: 30: 31] cm
(10 [10: 10½: 11: 11½: 12: 12] in)

27 [28.5: 30: 32: 33: 34.5: 35.5] cm
(10½ [11: 12: 12½: 13: 13½: 14] in)

summer

Designer: Martin Storey

main image page 11, 12 & 13

To fit age				
	12-18			months
		2	3	years
	5	6	6	x 50gm

(photographed in Apple Pips 482)

1 pair 2mm (no 14) (US 0) needles
1 pair 2¾mm (no 12) (US 2) needles

approx 500 small clear glass beads

30 sts and 38 rows to 10 cm measured over st st using 2¾mm (US 2) needles.

bead 1 = place a bead by taking yarn to RS of work and slipping bead up next to st just worked, slip next st purlwise from left needle to right needle and take yarn back to WS of work, leaving bead sitting in front of slipped st on RS.

Beading note: Before starting to knit, thread beads onto yarn. To do this, thread a fine sewing needle (one that will easily pass through the beads) with sewing thread. Knot ends of thread and then pass end of yarn through this loop. Thread a bead onto sewing thread and then gently slide it along and onto knitting yarn. Continue in this way until required number of beads are on yarn. Do not place beads on edge sts of rows as this will interfere with seaming.

Lower back
Using 2mm (US 0) needles cast on 132 [138: 141] sts.
Work in g st for 6 rows, ending with RS facing for next row.
Change to 2¾mm (US 2) needles.
Beg with a K row, work in st st until lower back meas 19 [19.5: 20] cm, ending with **WS** facing for next row.
Next row (WS): (P2tog) twice, (P1, P2tog) 42 [44: 45] times, P2tog. 87 [91: 93] sts.
Cast off all sts quite tightly.
Upper back
Using 2¾mm (US 2) needles cast on 87 [91: 93] sts.
Beg and ending rows as indicated and repeating the 44 row patt rep throughout, now work in patt from chart as folls:
Cont straight until upper back meas 8.5 [9.5: 10.5] cm, ending with RS facing for next row.

Shape armholes
Keeping patt correct, cast off 4 sts at beg of next 2 rows.
79 [83: 85] sts.
(**Note**: Armhole shaping is **NOT** shown on chart.)
Dec 1 st at each end of next and foll 3 alt rows. 71 [75: 77] sts.
Cont straight until armhole meas 12.5 [13: 13.5] cm, ending with RS facing for next row.
Shape shoulders and back neck
Next row (RS): Cast off 8 [8: 9] sts, patt until there are 11 [12: 12] sts on right needle and turn, leaving rem sts on a holder.
Work each side of neck separately.
Cast off 3 sts at beg of next row.
Cast off rem 8 [9: 9] sts.
With RS facing, slip centre 33 [35: 35] sts onto a holder, rejoin yarn to rem sts, patt to end.
Complete to match first side, reversing shapings.

Lower front
Work as given for lower back.
Upper front
Work as given for upper back until 16 rows less have been worked than on upper back to beg of shoulder shaping, ending with RS facing for next row.
Shape front neck
Next row (RS): Patt 23 [24: 25] sts and turn, leaving rem sts on a holder.
Work each side of neck separately.
Keeping patt correct, dec 1 st at neck edge of next 4 rows, then on foll 2 alt rows, then on foll 4th row. 16 [17: 18] sts.
Work 3 rows, ending with RS facing for next row.
Shape shoulder
Cast off 8 [8: 9] sts at beg of next row.
Work 1 row.
Cast off rem 8 [9: 9] sts.

With RS facing, slip centre 25 [27: 27] sts onto a holder, rejoin yarn to rem sts, patt to end.
Complete to match first side, reversing shapings.

SLEEVES

Using 2mm (US 0) needles cast on 47 [49: 49] sts.
Row 1 (RS): K1 [2: 2], *P3, K3, rep from * to last 4 [5: 5] sts, P3, K1 [2: 2].
Row 2: P1 [2: 2], *K3, P3, rep from * to last 4 [5: 5] sts, K3, P1 [2: 2].
These 2 rows form rib.
Work in rib for a further 6 rows, ending with RS facing for next row.
Change to 2¾mm (US 2) needles.
Beg and ending rows as indicated, now work in patt from chart as folls:

Inc 1 st at each end of 3rd and every foll 4th row to 75 [73: 69] sts, then on every foll – [6th: 6th] row until there are – [79: 81] sts, taking inc sts into patt.
Cont straight until sleeve meas 20 [22.5: 25] cm, ending with RS facing for next row.
Shape top
Keeping patt correct, cast off 4 sts at beg of next 2 rows.
67 [71: 73] sts.
Dec 1 st at each end of next and foll 3 alt rows, then on foll row, ending with RS facing for next row.
Cast off rem 57 [61: 63] sts.

MAKING UP

Press as described on the information page.
Join right shoulder seam using back stitch, or mattress stitch if preferred.

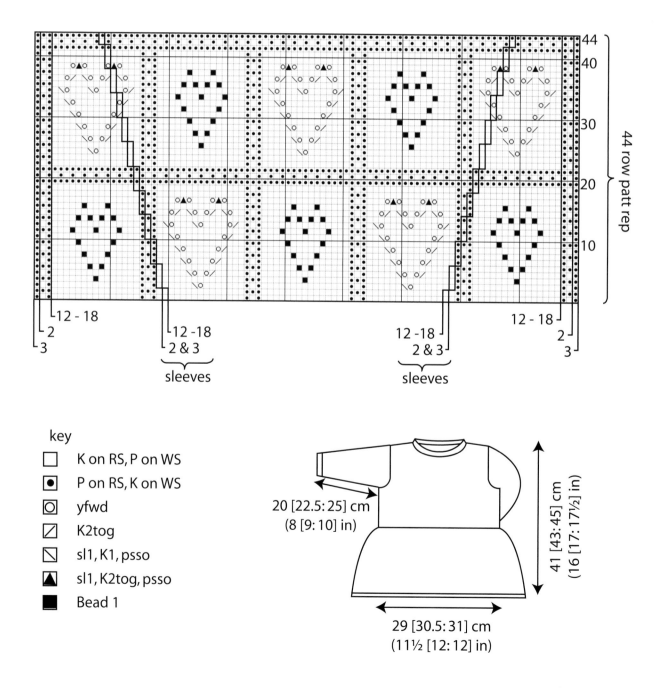

key

☐ K on RS, P on WS
⦿ P on RS, K on WS
Ⓞ yfwd
⟋ K2tog
⟍ sl1, K1, psso
▲ sl1, K2tog, psso
■ Bead 1

20 [22.5: 25] cm
(8 [9: 10] in)

41 [43: 45] cm
(16 [17: 17½] in)

29 [30.5: 31] cm
(11½ [12: 12] in)

Neckband

With RS facing and using 2mm (US 0) needles, pick up and knit 19 [20: 20] sts down left side of front neck, K across 25 [27: 27] sts on front holder, pick up and knit 19 [20: 20] sts up right side of front neck and 3 sts down right side of back neck, K across 33 [35: 35] sts on back holder, then pick up and knit 4 sts up left side of back neck.

103 [109: 109] sts.

Row 1 (WS): P2, ★K3, P3, rep from ★ to last 5 sts, K3, P2.

Row 2: K2, ★P3, K3, rep from ★ to last 5 sts, P3, K2.

These 2 rows form rib.

Work in rib for a further 6 rows, ending with **WS** facing for next row.

Using a 2¾mm (US 2) needle, cast off **loosely** in rib (on **WS**).

Join upper and lower backs and fronts by sewing cast-off edge of lower section to cast-on edge of upper section.

See information page for finishing instructions, setting in sleeves using the shallow set-in method.

rufus

Designer: Martin Storey

main image page 35 & 36

YARN

To fit age

	12-18	2	3	months years
Rowan Fine Milk Cotton				
A Opaque 506	4	5	5	x 50gm
B Midget Gem 497	1	1	1	x 50gm
C Liquorice 499	1	1	1	x 50gm

NEEDLES

1 pair 2mm (no 14) (US 0) needles
1 pair 2¾mm (no 12) (US 2) needles

BUTTONS

4 x BN1116 from Bedecked.
Please see information page for contact details.

TENSION

30 sts and 38 rows to 10 cm measured over st st using 2¾mm (US 2) needles.

BACK

Using 2mm (US 0) needles and yarn A cast on 87 [91: 93] sts.

Row 1 (RS): P0 [2: 3], ★K3, P3, rep from ★ to last 3 [5: 0] sts, K3 [3: 0], P0 [2: 0].

Row 2: K0 [2: 3], ★P3, K3, rep from ★ to last 3 [5: 0] sts, P3 [3: 0], K0 [2: 0].

These 2 rows form rib.

Work in rib for a further 14 rows, ending with RS facing for next row.

Change to 2¾mm (US 2) needles.

Beg with a K row, work in st st until back meas 17 [18: 20] cm, ending with RS facing for next row.

Shape raglan armholes

Cast off 3 sts at beg of next 2 rows. 81 [85: 87] sts.

Dec 1 st at each end of next and foll 4 [5: 6] alt rows, ending with **WS** facing for next row. 71 [73: 73] sts.

Next row (WS): P2 [3: 3], M1, (P6, M1) 11 times, P3 [4: 4]. 83 [85: 85] sts.

Beg and ending rows as indicated and using the **fairisle** technique as described on the information page, now work in patt from chart for yoke, which is worked entirely in st st beg with a K row, as folls:

Work 2 rows.

Dec 1 st at each end of next 2 rows.

Work 1 row.

Rep last 3 rows 3 times more, then first of these rows (a dec row) again, ending with **WS** facing for next row. 65 [67: 67] sts. (All 15 rows of chart are now completed.)

Break off contrasts and cont using yarn A **only**.

Next row (WS): P4 [5: 5], P2tog, (P3, P2tog) 11 times, P4 [5: 5]. 53 [55: 55] sts.

Beg with a K row, cont in st st, dec 1 st at each end of 3rd and

foll 9 alt rows. 33 [35: 35] sts.
Work 1 row, ending with RS facing for next row.
Cast off.

LEFT FRONT

Using 2mm (US 0) needles and yarn A cast on 44 [46: 47] sts.
Row 1 (RS): P0 [2: 3], ★K3, P3, rep from ★ to last 2 sts, K2.
Row 2: P2, K3, ★P3, K3, rep from ★ to last 3 [5: 0] sts, P3 [3: 0], K0 [2: 0].
These 2 rows form rib.
Work in rib for a further 14 rows, ending with RS facing for next row.
Change to 2¾mm (US 2) needles.
Beg with a K row, work in st st for 18 [20: 22] rows, ending with RS facing for next row.
Place chart
Next row (RS): K8 [9: 9], work next 29 sts as row 1 of chart for left front, K7 [8: 9].
Next row: P7 [8: 9], work next 29 sts as row 2 of chart for left front, P8 [9: 9].
These 2 rows set position of chart.
Cont as now set until all 28 rows of chart have been completed, ending with RS facing for next row.
Break off contrasts and cont using yarn A **only**.
Beg with a K row, work in st st until left front matches back to beg of raglan armhole shaping, ending with RS facing for next row.
Shape raglan armhole
Cast off 3 sts at beg of next row. 41 [43: 44] sts.
Work 1 row.
Dec 1 st at raglan armhole edge of next and foll 4 [5: 6] alt rows, ending with **WS** facing for next row. 36 [37: 37] sts.
Next row (WS): P3, M1, (P6, M1) 5 times, P3 [4: 4].
42 [43: 43] sts.
Beg and ending rows as indicated, now work in patt from chart for yoke as folls:
Work 2 rows.
Dec 1 st at raglan armhole edge of next 2 rows.
Work 1 row.
Rep last 3 rows 3 times more, then first of these rows (a dec row) again, ending with **WS** facing for next row. 33 [34: 34] sts.
(All 15 rows of chart are now completed.)
Break off contrasts and cont using yarn A **only**.
Next row (WS): (P3, P2tog) 6 times, P3 [4: 4]. 27 [28: 28] sts.
Beg with a K row, cont in st st, dec 1 st at raglan armhole edge of 3rd and foll 2 alt rows, ending with **WS** facing for next row. 24 [25: 25] sts.
Shape neck
Cast off 12 [13: 13] sts at beg of next row. 12 sts.
Dec 1 st at neck edge of next 5 rows, then on foll alt row **and at same time** dec 1 st at raglan armhole edge of next and foll 3 alt rows. 2 sts.
Work 1 row, ending with RS facing for next row.
Next row (RS): K2tog and fasten off.

RIGHT FRONT

Using 2mm (US 0) needles and yarn A cast on 44 [46: 47] sts.
Row 1 (RS): K2, P3, ★K3, P3, rep from ★ to last 3 [5: 0] sts, K3 [3: 0], P0 [2: 0].
Row 2: K0 [2: 3], ★P3, K3, rep from ★ to last 2 sts, P2.

These 2 rows form rib.
Work in rib for a further 14 rows, ending with RS facing for next row.
Change to 2¾mm (US 2) needles.
Beg with a K row, work in st st for 18 [20: 22] rows, ending with RS facing for next row.
Place chart
Next row (RS): K7 [8: 9], work next 29 sts as row 1 of chart for right front, K8 [9: 9].
Next row: P8 [9: 9], work next 29 sts as row 2 of chart for right front, P7 [8: 9].
These 2 rows set position of chart.
Complete to match left front, reversing shapings.

SLEEVES

Using 2mm (US 0) needles and yarn A cast on 45 [49: 49] sts.
Row 1 (RS): P0 [2: 2], K3, ★P3, K3, rep from ★ to last 0 [2: 2] sts, P0 [2: 2].
Row 2: K0 [2: 2], P3, ★K3, P3, rep from ★ to last 0 [2: 2] sts, K0 [2: 2].
These 2 rows form rib.
Work in rib for a further 14 rows, inc 1 st at each end of 7th of these rows and ending with RS facing for next row.
47 [51: 51] sts.
Change to 2¾mm (US 2) needles.
Beg with a K row, work in st st, shaping sides by inc 1 st at each end of next [3rd: 3rd] and every foll alt [4th: 4th] row to 55 [75: 71] sts, then on every foll 4th [6th: 6th] row until there are 77 [79: 81] sts.
Cont straight until sleeve meas 20 [22.5: 25] cm, ending with RS facing for next row.
Shape raglan
Cast off 3 sts at beg of next 2 rows. 71 [73: 75] sts.
Dec 1 st at each end of next and foll 4 [5: 6] alt rows, ending with **WS** facing for next row. 61 sts.
Next row (WS): P3, M1, (P5, M1) 11 times, P3. 73 sts.
Beg and ending rows as indicated, now work in patt from chart for yoke as folls:
Work 2 rows.
Dec 1 st at each end of next 2 rows.
Work 1 row.
Rep last 3 rows 3 times more, then first of these rows (a dec row) again, ending with **WS** facing for next row. 55 sts. (All 15 rows of chart are now completed.)
Break off contrasts and cont using yarn A **only**.
Next row (WS): P4, P2tog, (P2, P2tog) 11 times, P5. 43 sts.
Beg with a K row, cont in st st, dec 1 st at each end of 3rd and foll 6 alt rows. 29 sts.
Work 1 row, ending with RS facing for next row.
Left sleeve only
Dec 1 st at each end of next row, then cast off 6 sts at beg of foll row. 21 sts.
Dec 1 st at beg of next row, then cast off 7 sts at beg of foll row. 13 sts.
Dec 1 st at beg of next row, then cast off 6 sts at beg of foll row.
Right sleeve only
Cast off 7 sts at beg and dec 1 st at end of next row. 21 sts.
Work 1 row.
Rep last 2 rows once more. 13 sts.

Cast off 6 sts at beg and dec 1 st at end of next row.
Work 1 row.
Both sleeves
Cast off rem 6 sts.

MAKING UP

Press as described on the information page.
Join all raglan seams using back stitch, or mattress stitch if preferred.
Collar
With RS facing, using 2mm (US 0) needles and yarn A, beg and ending at front opening edges, pick up and knit 21 [22: 22] sts up right side of neck, 25 sts from top of right sleeve, 31 [35: 35] sts from back, 25 sts from top of left sleeve, then 21 [22: 22] sts down left side of neck. 123 [129: 129] sts.
Row 1 (WS): P3, *K3, P3, rep from * to end.
Row 2: K3, *P3, K3, rep from * to end.
These 2 rows form rib.
Work in rib until collar meas 6 cm from pick-up row, ending with RS facing for next row.
Cast off in rib.
Buttonhole border
With RS facing, using 2mm (US 0) needles and yarn A, pick up and knit 105 [105: 111] sts evenly down left front opening edge, from top of collar to cast-on edge.
Work in rib as given for collar for 5 rows, ending with RS facing for next row.
Row 6 (RS): Rib 5, *cast off 2 sts (to make a buttonhole – cast on 2 sts over these cast-off sts on next row), rib until there are 29 [29: 31] sts on right needle after cast-off, rep from *

twice more, cast off 2 sts (to make 4th buttonhole – cast on 2 sts over these cast-off sts on next row), rib to end.
Work in rib for a further 6 rows, ending with **WS** facing for next row.
Cast off in rib (on **WS**).
Button border
With RS facing, using 2mm (US 0) needles and yarn A, pick up and knit 105 [105: 111] sts evenly up right front opening edge, from cast-on edge to top of collar.
Work in rib as given for collar for 12 rows, ending with **WS** facing for next row.
Cast off in rib (on **WS**).
See information page for finishing instructions.

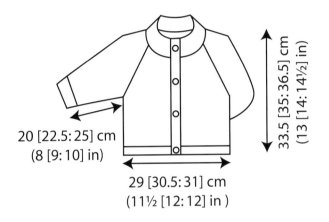

33.5 [35: 36.5] cm
(13 [14: 14½] in)

20 [22.5: 25] cm
(8 [9: 10] in)

29 [30.5: 31] cm
(11½ [12: 12] in)

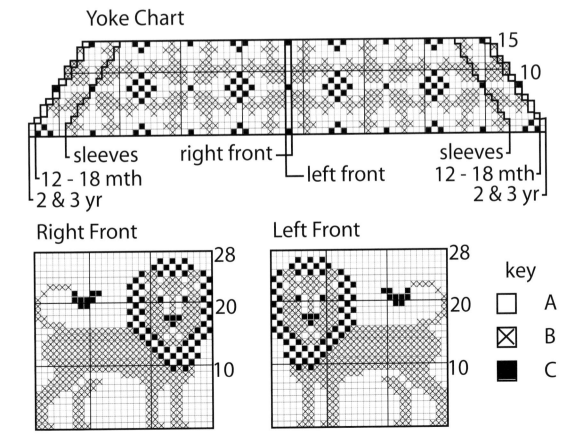

Yoke Chart

15

10

sleeves
right front
left front
sleeves

12 - 18 mth
2 & 3 yr

12 - 18 mth
2 & 3 yr

Right Front

28

20

10

Left Front

28

20

10

key

☐ A

☒ B

■ C

moonbeam

Designer: Martin Storey

main image page 33

YARN

To fit age

0-3	3-6	6-9	9-12	12-18	2	3	
3	3	4	4	4	5	5	x 50gm

(photographed in Cloud 805)

NEEDLES

1 pair 3¹/4mm (no 10) (US 3) needles
1 pair 4mm (no 8) (US 6) needles

TENSION

22 sts and 30 rows to 10 cm measured over st st using 4mm (US 6) needles.

BACK

Using 3¹/4mm (US 3) needles cast on 55 [57: 59: 61: 63: 65: 67] sts.
Row 1 (RS): K1, ★P1, K1, rep from ★ to end.
Row 2: P1, ★K1, P1, rep from ★ to end.
These 2 rows form rib.
Cont in rib for a further 12 [12: 14: 14: 16: 16: 16] rows, ending with RS facing for next row.
Change to 4mm (US 6) needles.
Beg with a K row, work in st st for 26 [28: 28: 34: 34: 36: 38] rows, ending with RS facing for next row. (Back should meas 13.5 [14: 14.5: 16.5: 17.5: 18: 18.5] cm.)
Shape raglan armholes
Cast off 2 sts at beg of next 2 rows. 51 [53: 55: 57: 59: 61: 63] sts.
Sizes 2 and 3 years only
Next row (RS): K2, sl 1, K1, psso, K to last 4 sts, K2tog, K2.
– [-: -: -: -: 59: 61] sts.
Next row: K2, P to last 2 sts, K2.
Next row: Knit.
Next row: K2, P to last 2 sts, K2.
All sizes
Next row (RS): K2, sl 1, K1, psso, K to last 4 sts, K2tog, K2.
Next row: K2, P to last 2 sts, K2.
Rep last 2 rows 15 [16: 17: 17: 18: 17: 18] times more, ending with RS facing for next row.
Cast off rem 19 [19: 19: 21: 21: 23: 23] sts.

LEFT FRONT

Using 3¹/4mm (US 3) needles cast on 43 [45: 47: 49: 51: 53: 55] sts.
Work in rib as given for back for 14 [14: 16: 16: 18: 18: 18] rows, ending with RS facing for next row.
Change to 4mm (US 6) needles.

Beg with a K row, work in st st for 2 rows, ending with RS facing for next row.
Shape front slope
Dec 1 st at end of next and foll 11 [12: 12: 15: 15: 16: 17] alt rows. 31 [32: 34: 33: 35: 36: 37] sts.
Work 1 row, ending with RS facing for next row.
Shape raglan armhole
Cast off 2 sts at beg and dec 1 st at end of next row.
28 [29: 31: 30: 32: 33: 34] sts.
Work 1 row.
Working all raglan armhole decreases as set by back, dec 1 st at raglan armhole edge of next and 0 [0: 0: 0: 0: 1: 1] foll 4th rows, then on foll 11 [11: 12: 12: 13: 12: 13] alt rows **and at same time** dec 1 st at front slope edge of next and foll 11 [11: 12: 11: 12: 13: 12] alt rows, then on 0 [0: 0: 0: 0: 0: 1] foll 4th row.
4 [5: 5: 5: 5: 5: 5] sts.
Work 1 row, ending with RS facing for next row.
Size 0-3 months only
Next row: K1, sl 1, K2tog, psso. 2 sts.
Sizes 3-6, 6-9, 9-12 and 12-18 months, and 2 and 3 years only
Next row: K2, sl 1, K2tog, psso. 3 sts.
Next row: P1, K2.
Next row: K1, sl 1, K1, psso. 2 sts.
All sizes
Next row (WS): K2.
Next row: K2tog and fasten off.

RIGHT FRONT

Using 3¹/4mm (US 3) needles cast on 43 [45: 47: 49: 51: 53: 55] sts.
Work in rib as given for back for 14 [14: 16: 16: 18: 18: 18] rows, ending with RS facing for next row.
Change to 4mm (US 6) needles.
Beg with a K row, work in st st for 2 rows, ending with RS facing for next row.

Shape front slope

Dec 1 st at beg of next and foll 11 [12: 12: 15: 15: 16: 17] alt rows. 31 [32: 34: 33: 35: 36: 37] sts.

Complete to match left front, reversing shapings.

SLEEVES

Using 3¼mm (US 3) needles cast on 29 [31: 31: 33: 33: 35: 35] sts.

Work in rib as given for back for 8 [8: 10: 10: 12: 12: 12] rows, ending with RS facing for next row.

Change to 4mm (US 6) needles.

Beg with a K row, work in st st, shaping sides by inc 1 st at each end of next [next: next: next: next: 3rd: 3rd] and foll 2 [0: 0: 0: 0: 0: 0] rows, then on foll 8 [7: 6: 3: 3: 0: 0] alt rows, then on 0 [3: 5: 7: 8: 11: 10] foll 4th rows, then on 0 [0: 0: 0: 0: 0: 2] foll 6th rows. 51 [53: 55: 55: 57: 59: 61] sts.

Cont straight until sleeve meas 11.5 [14: 16.5: 18.5: 20.5: 23: 25.5] cm, ending with RS facing for next row.

Shape raglan

Cast off 2 sts at beg of next 2 rows.

47 [49: 51: 51: 53: 55: 57] sts.

Working all raglan decreases as given for back raglan armholes, dec 1 st at each end of next and every foll alt row until 21 sts rem.

Work 1 row, ending with RS facing for next row.

Left sleeve only

Dec 1 st at each end of next row, then cast off 4 sts at beg of foll row. 15 sts.

Dec 1 st at beg of next row, then cast off 5 sts at beg of foll row. 9 sts.

Dec 1 st at beg of next row, then cast off 4 sts at beg of foll row.

Right sleeve only

Cast off 5 sts at beg and dec 1 st at end of next row. 15 sts.

Work 1 row.

Rep last 2 rows once more. 9 sts.

Cast off 4 sts at beg and dec 1 st at end of next row.

Work 1 row.

Both sleeves

Cast off rem 4 sts.

MAKING UP

Press as described on the information page.

Join all raglan seams using back stitch, or mattress stitch if preferred.

Front band

Using 3¼mm (US 3) needles cast on 6 sts.

Row 1 (RS): Sl 1, K5.

Rep this row until band, when slightly stretched and beg and ending at cast-on edges, fits up entire right front opening edge, across top of right sleeve, then back neck, then left sleeve, then down entire left front opening edge, ending with **WS** facing for next row.

Cast off knitwise (on **WS**).

Slip stitch band in place.

Ties (make 2)

Using 3¼mm (US 3) needles cast on 6 sts.

Row 1 (RS): Sl 1, K5.

Rep this row until tie meas 29 [30: 31: 32: 33: 34: 35] cm, ending with **WS** facing for next row.

Cast off knitwise (on **WS**).

Sew one end of each tie to front opening edge just about beg of front slope shaping.

See information page for finishing instructions, leaving a small opening in right side seam level with tie.

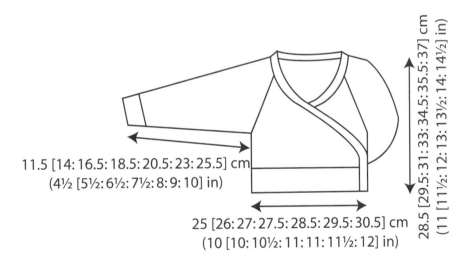

11.5 [14: 16.5: 18.5: 20.5: 23: 25.5] cm
(4½ [5½: 6½: 7½: 8: 9: 10] in)

25 [26: 27: 27.5: 28.5: 29.5: 30.5] cm
(10 [10: 10½: 11: 11: 11½: 12] in)

28.5 [29.5: 31: 33: 34.5: 35.5: 37] cm
(11 [11½: 12: 13: 13½: 14: 14½] in)

prudence

Designer: Martin Storey

main image page 34, 35 & 36

YARN

To fit age	12-18			months
		2	3	years
Rowan Fine Milk Cotton				
A Sepia 501	3	4	4	x 50gm
B Snow 493	2	2	2	x 50gm

NEEDLES

1 pair 2mm (no 14) (US 0) needles
1 pair 2¾mm (no 12) (US 2) needles
2 double-pointed 2mm (no 14) (US 0) needles

BUTTONS

6 x BN1150 (small) from Bedecked.
Please see information page for contact details.

TENSION

34 sts and 34 rows to 10 cm measured over patterned st st using 2¾mm (US 2) needles.

BACK

Using 2mm (US 0) needles and yarn A cast on 87 [91: 93] sts.
Row 1 (RS): P0 [2: 3], ★K3, P3, rep from ★ to last 3 [5: 0] sts, K3 [3: 0], P0 [2: 0].
Row 2: K0 [2: 3], ★P3, K3, rep from ★ to last 3 [5: 0] sts, P3 [3: 0], K0 [2: 0].
These 2 rows form rib.
Work in rib for a further 17 rows, ending with **WS** facing for next row.
Row 20 (WS): Rib 5 [1: 2], M1, (rib 7 [8: 8], M1) 11 times, rib 5 [2: 3]. 99 [103: 105] sts.
Change to 2¾mm (US 2) needles.
Beg and ending rows as indicated, using the **fairisle** technique as described on the information page, now work in patt from chart for body, which is worked entirely in st st beg with a K row, as folls:
Cont straight until chart row 42 [44: 46] has been completed, ending with RS facing for next row. (Back should meas 17.5 [18: 18.5] cm.)
Shape armholes
Keeping patt correct, cast off 5 sts at beg of next 2 rows. 89 [93: 95] sts.
Dec 1 st at each end of next and foll 3 alt rows. 81 [85: 87] sts.
Working rem 23 [21: 19] rows of chart and then completing back in st st using yarn A **only**, cont as folls:
Cont straight until armhole meas 13 [13.5: 14] cm, ending with RS facing for next row.
Shape shoulders and back neck
Next row (RS): Cast off 9 [9: 10] sts, K until there are 12 [13: 13] sts on right needle and turn, leaving rem sts on a holder.
Work each side of neck separately.

Cast off 3 sts at beg of next row.
Cast off rem 9 [10: 10] sts.
With RS facing, rejoin yarn to rem sts, cast off centre 39 [41: 41] sts, K to end.
Complete to match first side, reversing shapings.

LEFT FRONT

Using 2mm (US 0) needles and yarn A cast on 45 [47: 48] sts.
Row 1 (RS): P0 [2: 3], ★K3, P3, rep from ★ to last 3 sts, K3.
Row 2: ★P3, K3, rep from ★ to last 3 [5: 0] sts, P3 [3: 0], K0 [2: 0].
These 2 rows form rib.
Work in rib for a further 17 rows, ending with **WS** facing for next row.
Row 20 (WS): Rib 4 [5: 4], M1, (rib 9 [9: 10], M1) 4 times, rib 5 [6: 4]. 50 [52: 53] sts.
Change to 2¾mm (US 2) needles.
Beg and ending rows as indicated, now work in patt from chart for body as folls:
Cont straight until chart row 42 [44: 46] has been completed, ending with RS facing for next row.
Shape armhole
Keeping patt correct, cast off 5 sts at beg of next row. 45 [47: 48] sts.
Work 1 row.
Dec 1 st at armhole edge of next and foll 3 alt rows. 41 [43: 44] sts.
Working rem 23 [21: 19] rows of chart and then completing left front in st st using yarn A **only**, cont as folls:
Cont straight until 13 rows less have been worked than on back to beg of shoulder shaping, ending with **WS** facing for next row.
Shape neck
Keeping patt correct, cast off 13 [14: 14] sts at beg of next row, then 5 sts at beg of foll alt row. 23 [24: 25] sts.
Dec 1 st at neck edge of next 3 rows, then on foll 2 alt rows.

18 [19: 20] sts.
Work 3 rows, ending with RS facing for next row.
Shape shoulder
Cast off 9 [9: 10] sts at beg of next row.
Work 1 row.
Cast off rem 9 [10: 10] sts.

RIGHT FRONT
Using 2mm (US 0) needles and yarn A cast on 45 [47: 48] sts.
Row 1 (RS): ★K3, P3, rep from ★ to last 3 [5: 0] sts, K3 [3: 0], P0 [2: 0].
Row 2: K0 [2: 3], ★P3, K3, rep from ★ to last 3 sts, P3.
These 2 rows form rib.
Complete to match left front, reversing shapings.

SLEEVES
Using 2mm (US 0) needles and yarn A cast on 45 [49: 49] sts.
Row 1 (RS): P0 [2: 2], K3, ★P3, K3, rep from ★ to last 0 [2: 2] sts, P0 [2: 2].
Row 2: K0 [2: 2], P3, ★K3, P3, rep from ★ to last 0 [2: 2] sts, K0 [2: 2].
These 2 rows form rib.
Work in rib for a further 17 rows, ending with **WS** facing for next row.
Row 20 (WS): Rib 1 [3: 3], M1, (rib 6, M1) 7 times, rib 2 [4: 4]. 53 [57: 57] sts.
Change to 2¾mm (US 2) needles.
Beg and ending rows as indicated, using the **fairisle** technique as described on the information page, now work in patt from chart for sleeve, which is worked entirely in st st beg with a K row, as folls:
(**Note:** Work all 58 rows of chart and then complete sleeve in st st using yarn A **only**.)
Inc 1 st at each end of 3rd and foll 9 [5: 5] alt rows, then on 7 [11: 13] foll 4th rows, taking inc sts into patt. 87 [91: 95] sts.
Work 3 rows, ending with RS facing for next row. (Sleeve should meas 19 [21.5: 24] cm.)
Shape top
Keeping patt correct, cast off 5 sts at beg of next 2 rows. 77 [81: 85] sts.
Dec 1 st at each end of next and foll 3 alt rows, then on foll row, ending with RS facing for next row.
Cast off rem 67 [71: 75] sts.

MAKING UP
Press as described on the information page.
Join both shoulder seams using back stitch, or mattress stitch if preferred.
Neckband
With RS facing, using 2mm (US 0) needles and yarn A, beg and ending at front opening edges, pick up and knit 29 sts up right side of neck, 41 sts from back, then 29 sts down left side of neck. 99 sts.
Row 1 (WS): P3, ★K3, P3, rep from ★ to end.
Row 2: K3, ★P3, K3, rep from ★ to end.
These 2 rows form rib.
Work in rib for a further 3 rows, ending with RS facing for next row.

Row 6 (eyelet row) (RS): Rib 6, (K2tog, yfwd, rib 10) 7 times, K2tog, yfwd, rib 7.
Work in rib for a further 6 rows, ending with **WS** facing for next row.
Cast off **loosely** in rib (on **WS**).
Buttonhole border
With RS facing, using 2mm (US 0) needles and yarn A, pick up and knit 105 [105: 111] sts evenly up right front opening edge, from cast-on edge to top of neckband.
Work in rib as given for neckband for 3 rows, ending with RS facing for next row.
Row 4 (RS): Rib 4 [4: 5], ★cast off 2 sts (to make a buttonhole – cast on 2 sts over these cast-off sts on next row), rib until there are 17 [17: 18] sts on right needle after cast-off, rep from ★ 4 times more, cast off 2 sts (to make 6th buttonhole – cast on 2 sts over these cast-off sts on next row), rib to end.
Work in rib for a further 5 rows, ending with RS facing for next row.
Cast off in rib.
Button border
With RS facing, using 2mm (US 0) needles and yarn A, pick up and knit 105 [105: 111] sts evenly down left front opening edge, from top of neckband to cast-on edge.
Work in rib as given for neckband for 9 rows, ending with RS facing for next row.
Cast off in rib.
See information page for finishing instructions, setting in sleeves using the shallow set-in method.
Neck tie
Using double-pointed 2mm (US 0) needles and yarn A cast on 3 sts.
Row 1 (RS): K3, ★without turning slip these 3 sts to opposite end of needle and bring yarn to opposite end of work pulling it quite tightly across **WS** of work, K these 3 sts again, rep from ★ until tie is 60 cm long.
Cast off.
Using photograph as a guide, thread neck tie through eyelet holes of neckband, secure at back of neck (neck ties may not be suitable for young children). Using yarn A, make two 3 cm diameter pompons and attach one to each end of tie.

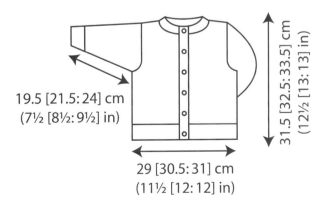

19.5 [21.5: 24] cm
(7½ [8½: 9½] in)

31.5 [32.5: 33.5] cm
(12½ [13: 13] in)

29 [30.5: 31] cm
(11½ [12: 12] in)

Body Chart

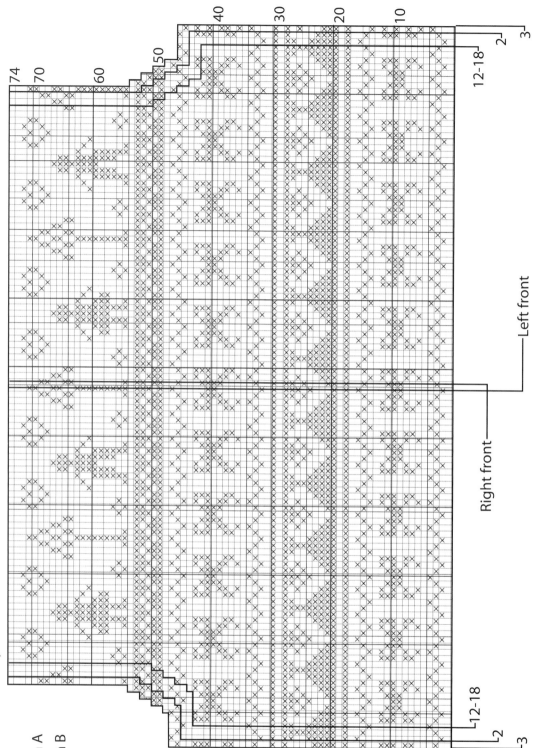

Key

☐ K on RS, P on WS in A

☒ K on RS, P on WS in B

Sleeve Chart

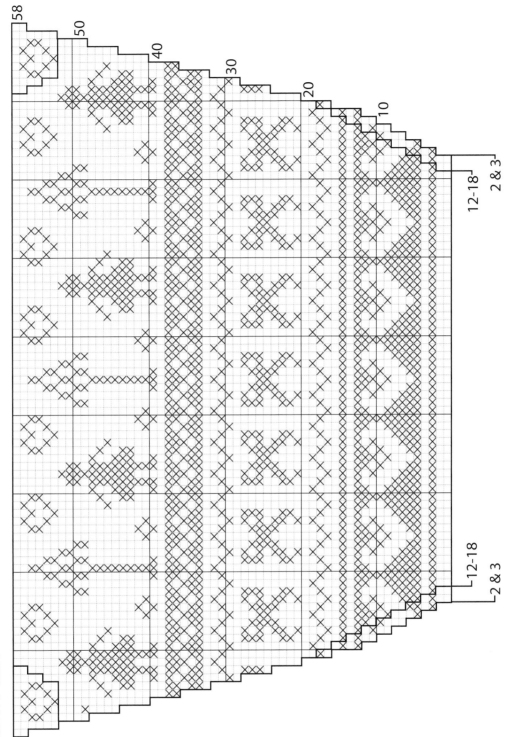

Designer: Martin Storey

main image page 4 & 5

YARN

To fit age

		12-18			months
			2	3	years

Rowan Cashsoft DK and Cashsoft Baby DK

A	Cash Bloom 520	2	2	2	x 50gm
B	Cash Lime 509	1	1	1	x 50gm
C	Cash Sweet 501	1	1	1	x 50gm
D	Baby Horseradish 801	1	1	2	x 50gm
E	Baby Sage 818	1	1	1	x 50gm

NEEDLES

1 pair 3¼mm (no 10) (US 3) needles
1 pair 4mm (no 8) (US 6) needles

TENSION

26½ sts and 25 rows to 10 cm measured over patterned st st using 4mm (US 6) needles.

BACK

Using 4mm (US 6) needles and yarn A cast on 65 [69: 71] sts.
Beg with a K row, work in st st for 2 rows, ending with RS facing for next row.
Beg and ending rows as indicated, using the **fairisle** technique as described on the information page and repeating the 38 row patt rep throughout, now work in patt from chart, which is worked entirely in st st beg with a K row, as folls:
Inc 1 st at each end of 3rd and 2 [1: 0] foll 4th rows, then on 1 [2: 3] foll 6th rows, taking inc sts into patt. 73 [77: 79] sts.
Work 5 rows, ending with RS facing for next row. (Back should meas 9.5 [10.5: 11] cm.)

Shape armholes
Keeping patt correct, cast off 3 sts at beg of next 2 rows.
67 [71: 73] sts.
Dec 1 st at each end of next 1 [3: 3] rows, then on foll alt row, then on foll 4th row. 61 [61: 63] sts.
Cont straight until armhole meas 12 [12.5: 13] cm, ending with RS facing for next row.

Shape shoulders and back neck
Next row (RS): Cast off 6 [5: 6] sts, patt until there are 9 sts on right needle and turn, leaving rem sts on a holder.
Work each side of neck separately.
Cast off 3 sts at beg of next row.
Cast off rem 6 sts.
With RS facing, slip centre 31 [33: 33] sts onto a holder, rejoin yarn to rem sts, patt to end.
Complete to match first side, reversing shapings.

FRONT

Work as given for back until 10 rows less have been worked than on back to beg of shoulder shaping, ending with RS facing for next row.

Shape front neck
Next row (RS): Patt 18 [17: 18] sts and turn, leaving rem sts on a holder.
Work each side of neck separately.
Keeping patt correct, dec 1 st at neck edge of next 4 rows, then on foll 2 alt rows. 12 [11: 12] sts.
Work 1 row, ending with RS facing for next row.

Shape shoulder
Cast off 6 [5: 6] sts at beg of next row.
Work 1 row.
Cast off rem 6 sts.
With RS facing, slip centre 25 [27: 27] sts onto a holder, rejoin yarn to rem sts, patt to end.
Complete to match first side, reversing shapings.

SLEEVES

Using 3¼mm (US 3) needles and yarn A cast on 47 [49: 51] sts.
Row 1 (RS): K1, *P1, K1, rep from * to end.
Row 2: P1, *K1, P1, rep from * to end.
Rep last 2 rows twice more, ending with RS facing for next row.
Change to 4mm (US 6) needles.
Beg with a K row, work in st st for 2 rows, ending with RS facing for next row.
Beg and ending rows as indicated, now work in patt from chart as folls:
Inc 1 st at each end of next and foll 4 alt rows, taking inc sts into patt. 57 [59: 61] sts.
Work 1 row, ending with RS facing for next row.

Shape top
Keeping patt correct, cast off 3 sts at beg of next 2 rows.
51 [53: 55] sts.
Dec 1 st at each end of next 3 rows, then on every foll alt row

until 37 sts rem, then on foll 7 rows, ending with RS facing for next row.
Cast off rem 23 sts.

Press as described on the information page.
Join right shoulder seam using back stitch, or mattress stitch if preferred.

Neckband

With RS facing, using 3¼mm (US 3) needles and yarn A, pick up and knit 12 sts down left side of front neck, K across 25 [27: 27] sts on front holder dec 3 sts evenly, pick up and knit 12 sts up right side of front neck and 2 sts down right side of back neck, K across 31 [33: 33] sts on back holder dec 3 sts evenly, then pick up and knit 2 sts up left side of back neck.
78 [82: 82] sts.
Work in g st for 6 rows, ending with **WS** facing for next row.
Using a 4mm (US 6) needle, cast off **loosely** knitwise (on **WS**).
See information page for finishing instructions, setting in sleeves using the set-in method.

Hem edging

Using 3¼mm (US 3) needles and yarn A cast on 3 sts.
Row 1 (WS): P3.
Row 2: K1, yfwd, K1 tbl, K1. 4 sts.

Row 3: P2, (K1, P1, K1, P1) all into yfwd of previous row, P1. 7 sts.
Row 4: Cast off 4 sts (one st on right needle), K1 tbl, P1. 3 sts.
These 4 rows form patt.
Cont in patt until hem edging fits neatly around entire back and front cast-on edges, ending after patt row 4 and with **WS** facing for next row.
Cast off (on **WS**).
Join ends of edging, then neatly slip stitch edging in place, matching edging seam to base of left side seam.

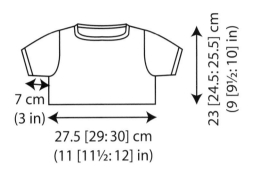

7 cm
(3 in)

27.5 [29: 30] cm
(11 [11½: 12] in)

23 [24.5: 25.5] cm
(9 [9½: 10] in)

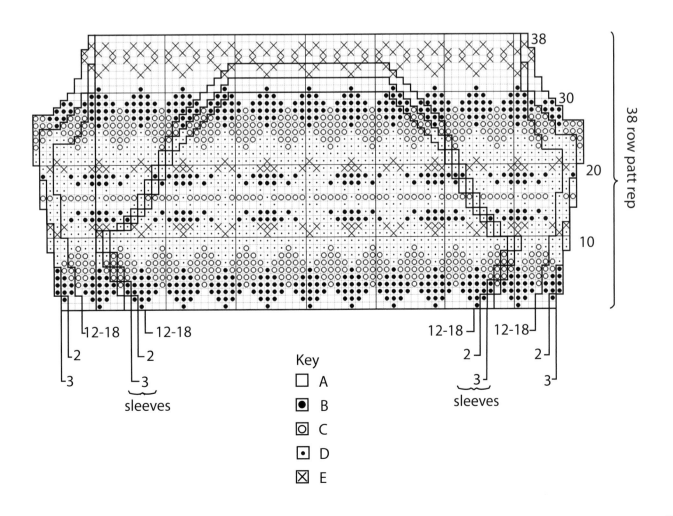

38 row patt rep

Key
☐ A
⊡ B
◉ C
⊡ D
☒ E

Designer: Martin Storey

main image page 28 & 29

YARN

To fit age

| 0-3 | 3-6 | 6-9 | 9-12 | 12-18 | | | months |
| | | | | | 2 | 3 | years |

Rowan Cashsoft DK

| | 3 | 3 | 3 | 3 | 4 | 4 | 4 | x 50gm |

(photographed in Lime 509 and Poppy 512)

NEEDLES

1 pair 3¼mm (no 10) (US 3) needles
1 pair 4mm (no 8) (US 6) needles

BUTTONS

3 x BN1150 (small) from Bedecked.
Please see information page for contact details.

TENSION

22 sts and 30 rows to 10 cm measured over st st using 4mm (US 6) needles.

SPECIAL ABBREVIATIONS

dec2K = slip next 2 sts as though to K2tog, K1, then pass 2 slipped sts over; **dec2P** = P1 and slip this st back onto left needle, lift next 2 sts on left needle over this st and off left needle, then slip st back onto right needle.

BACK

Using 3¼mm (US 3) needles cast on 55 [57: 59: 61: 63: 67: 69] sts.
Row 1 (RS): Knit.
Row 2: Purl.
Rows 3 to 5: Knit.
Row 6: *P2tog, yrn, rep from * to last st, P1.
Rows 7 and 8: Knit.
These 8 rows complete border.
Change to 4mm (US 6) needles.
Beg with a K row, work in st st until back meas 13.5 [14.5: 15.5: 16.5: 17.5: 18.5: 19.5] cm, ending with RS facing for next row.
Shape armholes
Cast off 3 sts at beg of next 2 rows. 49 [51: 53: 55: 57: 61: 63] sts.
Dec 1 st at each end of next 3 rows.
43 [45: 47: 49: 51: 55: 57] sts.
Work 9 [9: 11: 13: 15: 15: 17] rows, ending with RS facing for next row.
Divide for back opening
Next row (RS): K20 [21: 22: 23: 24: 26: 27] and turn, leaving rem sts on a holder.
Work each side of neck separately.
Work 19 rows, ending with RS facing for next row. (Armhole should meas 11.5 [11.5: 12: 12.5: 13.5: 13.5: 14] cm.)
Shape shoulder and back neck
Next row (RS): Cast off 4 [4: 4: 5: 5: 6: 6] sts, K until there are

7 [7: 8: 8: 9: 9: 10] sts on right needle and turn, leaving rem 9 [10: 10: 10: 10: 11: 11] sts on a second holder.
Cast off 3 sts at beg of next row.
Cast off rem 4 [4: 5: 5: 6: 6: 7] sts.
With RS facing, rejoin yarn to rem sts on first holder, cast off centre 3 sts, K to end.
Complete to match first side, reversing shapings.

FRONT

Work as given for back until 4 [6: 4: 2: 2: 2: 0] rows less have been worked than on back to beg of armhole shaping, ending with RS facing for next row.
0-3, 3-6, 6-9, 9-12 and 12-18 months and 2 years sizes only
Place star motif
Next row (RS): K17 [18: 19: 20: 21: 23: -], work next 21 sts as row 1 of chart, K to end.
Next row: P17 [18: 19: 20: 21: 23: -], work next 21 sts as row 2 of chart, P to end.
These 2 rows set the sts – centre 21 sts from chart with all other sts still in st st.
Keeping sts correct, work 2 [4: 2: 0: 0: 0: -] rows, ending with RS facing for next row.
Shape armholes
Cast off 3 sts at beg of next 2 rows. 49 [51: 53: 55: 57: 61: -] sts.
3 years size only
Place star motif and shape armholes
Next row (RS): Cast off 3 sts, K until there are 21 sts on right needle, work next 21 sts as row 1 of chart, K to end.
Next row: Cast off 3 sts, P until there are 21 sts on right needle, work next 21 sts as row 2 of chart, P to end. 63 sts.
These 2 rows set the sts – centre 21 sts from chart with all other sts still in st st.
All sizes
Keeping sts correct, dec 1 st at each end of next 3 rows.

43 [45: 47: 49: 51: 55: 57] sts.

Work 13 [11: 13: 15: 15: 15: 17] rows, ending with RS facing for next row. All 22 rows of chart now completed.

Now working all sts in st st, cont as folls:

Work 6 rows, ending with RS facing for next row.

Shape front neck

Next row (RS): K14 [15: 16: 17: 19: 20: 21] and turn, leaving rem sts on a holder.

Work each side of neck separately.

Dec 1 st at neck edge of next 4 rows, then on foll 2 [3: 3: 3: 4: 4: 4] alt rows. 8 [8: 9: 10: 11: 12: 13] sts.

Work 1 row, ending with RS facing for next row.

Shape shoulder

Cast off 4 [4: 4: 5: 5: 6: 6] sts at beg of next row.

Work 1 row.

Cast off rem 4 [4: 5: 5: 6: 6: 7] sts.

With RS facing, slip centre 15 [15: 15: 15: 13: 15: 15] sts onto a holder, rejoin yarn to rem sts, K to end.

Complete to match first side, reversing shapings.

SLEEVES

Using 3¹/4mm (US 3) needles cast on 29 [31: 31: 33: 33: 35: 35] sts.

Row 1 (RS): Knit.

Row 2: Purl.

Rows 3 to 5: Knit, inc 1 st at each end of first [first: first: 3rd: 3rd: 3rd: 3rd] of these rows and foll 1 [1: 0: 0: 0: 0: 0] alt row. 33 [35: 33: 35: 35: 37: 37] sts.

Row 6: ⋆P2tog, yrn, rep from ⋆ to last st, P1.

Rows 7 and 8: Knit, inc 1 [1: 1: 0: 0: 0: 0] st at each end of first of these rows. 35 [37: 35: 35: 35: 37: 37] sts.

These 8 rows complete border.

Change to 4mm (US 6) needles.

Beg with a K row, work in st st, shaping sides by inc 1 st at each end of next [3rd: 3rd: next: next: next: next] and every foll alt [4th: 4th: 4th: 4th: 4th: 4th] row to 41 [51: 53: 51: 51: 45: 43] sts, then on every foll 4th [–: –: 6th: 6th: 6th: 6th] row until there are 49 [–: –: 55: 57: 59: 61] sts.

Cont straight until sleeve meas 12 [14.5: 17: 19: 21: 23.5: 26] cm, ending with RS facing for next row.

Shape top

Cast off 3 sts at beg of next 2 rows. 43 [45: 47: 49: 51: 53: 55] sts.

Dec 1 st at each end of next and foll 2 alt rows, then on foll row, ending with RS facing for next row.

Cast off rem 35 [37: 39: 41: 43: 45: 47] sts.

MAKING UP

Press as described on the information page.

Join both shoulder seams using back stitch, or mattress stitch if preferred.

Buttonhole border

With RS facing and using 3¹/4mm (US 3) needles, pick up and knit 15 sts evenly up left side of back opening, from cast-off sts at base of opening to sts left on holder at neck edge.

Work in g st for 1 row, ending with RS facing for next row.

Row 2 (RS): K3, (K2tog, yfwd, K4) twice.

Work in g st for a further 2 rows, ending with **WS** facing for next row.

Cast off knitwise (on **WS**).

Button border

With RS facing and using 3¹/4mm (US 3) needles, pick up and knit 15 sts evenly down right side of back opening, from sts left on holder at neck edge to cast-off sts at base of opening.

Work in g st for 4 rows, ending with **WS** facing for next row.

Cast off knitwise (on **WS**).

Lay buttonhole band over button band and sew row-end edges of bands to cast-off sts at base of opening.

Neckband

With RS facing and using 3¹/4mm (US 3) needles, pick up and knit 3 sts across top of buttonhole band, K9 [10: 10: 10: 10: 11: 11] sts on left back holder, pick up and knit 4 sts up left side of back neck and 11 [13: 13: 13: 15: 15: 15] sts down left side of front neck, K15 [15: 15: 15: 13: 15: 15] sts on front holder, pick up and knit 11 [13: 13: 13: 15: 15: 15] sts up right side of front neck and 4 sts down right side of back neck, K9 [10: 10: 10: 10: 11: 11] sts on right back holder, then pick up and knit 3 sts

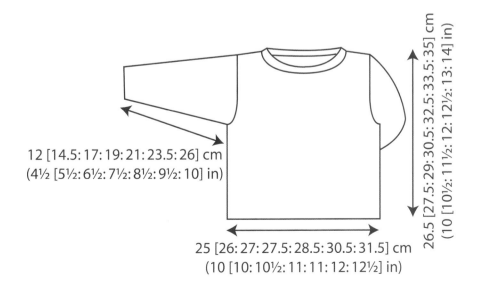

12 [14.5: 17: 19: 21: 23.5: 26] cm
(4½ [5½: 6½: 7½: 8½: 9½: 10] in)

26.5 [27.5: 29: 30.5: 32.5: 33.5: 35] cm
(10 [10½: 11½: 12: 12½: 13: 14] in)

25 [26: 27: 27.5: 28.5: 30.5: 31.5] cm
(10 [10: 10½: 11: 11: 12: 12½] in)

across top of button band. 69 [75: 75: 75: 77: 81: 81] sts.
Work in g st for 1 row, ending with RS facing for next row.
Row 2 (RS): K1, K2tog, yfwd, K to end.
Work in g st for a further 2 rows, ending with **WS** facing for

next row.
Cast off knitwise (on **WS**).
See information page for finishing instructions, setting in sleeves using the shallow set-in method.

skye ಎ

Designer: Martin Storey

main image page 26 & 27

YARN
To fit age
   0-3   3-6   6-9   9-12 12-18   months
Rowan Handknit Cotton
    4   4   5   5   5   x 50gm
(photographed in Aubergine 348)

NEEDLES
1 pair 3¼mm (no 10) (US 3) needles
1 pair 4mm (no 8) (US 6) needles

BUTTONS
3 x BN1150 (small) from Bedecked.
Please see information page for contact details.

TENSION
20 sts and 28 rows to 10 cm measured over st st using 4mm (US 6) needles.

BACK
Using 3¼mm (US 3) needles cast on 70 [72: 74: 76: 78] sts.
Work in g st for 4 rows, ending with RS facing for next row.
Change to 4mm (US 6) needles.
Beg with a K row, work in st st for 2 [2: 2: 4: 4] rows, ending with RS facing for next row.
Next row (RS): K2, sl 1, K1, psso, K8, sl 1, K1, psso, K to last 14 sts, K2tog, K8, K2tog, K2.
Work 7 rows.
Rep last 8 rows 3 times more, then first of these rows (the dec row) again. 50 [52: 54: 56: 58] sts.
Work 1 [3: 5: 5: 7] rows, ending with RS facing for next row.
(Back should meas 14.5 [15: 15.5: 16.5: 17] cm.)
Shape raglan armholes
Cast off 2 sts at beg of next 2 rows. 46 [48: 50: 52: 54] sts.
Next row (RS): K2, sl 1, K1, psso, K to last 4 sts, K2tog, K2.
Next row: Purl.
Next row: Knit.
Next row: Purl.
Rep last 4 rows 0 [1: 1: 2: 2] times more. 44 [44: 46: 46: 48] sts.

Next row (RS): K2, sl 1, K1, psso, K to last 4 sts, K2tog, K2.
Next row: Purl.
Rep last 2 rows 12 [11: 12: 11: 12] times more, ending with RS facing for next row.
Cast off rem 18 [20: 20: 22: 22] sts.

LEFT FRONT
Using 3¼mm (US 3) needles cast on 35 [36: 37: 38: 39] sts.
Work in g st for 4 rows, ending with RS facing for next row.
Change to 4mm (US 6) needles.
Beg with a K row, work in st st for 2 [2: 2: 4: 4] rows, ending with RS facing for next row.
Next row (RS): K2, sl 1, K1, psso, K8, sl 1, K1, psso, K to end.
Work 7 rows.
Rep last 8 rows 3 times more, then first of these rows (the dec row) again. 25 [26: 27: 28: 29] sts.
Work 1 [3: 5: 5: 7] rows, ending with RS facing for next row.
Shape raglan armhole
Cast off 2 sts at beg of next row. 23 [24: 25: 26: 27] sts.
Work 1 row.
Working all raglan armhole decreases as set by back raglan armholes, dec 1 st at raglan armhole edge of next and 1 [2: 2: 3: 3] foll 4th rows, then on foll 6 [5: 6: 5: 6] alt rows, ending with **WS** facing for next row. 15 [16: 16: 17: 17] sts.

Shape neck

Cast off 5 [6: 6: 7: 7] sts at beg of next row. 10 sts.
Dec 1 st at neck edge of next 4 rows, ending with RS facing for next row **and at same time** dec 1 st at raglan armhole edge of next and foll alt row. 4 sts.
Next row (RS): K1, sl 1, K2tog, psso.
Next row: P2.
Next row: K2tog and fasten off.

RIGHT FRONT

Using 3¼mm (US 3) needles cast on 35 [36: 37: 38: 39] sts.
Work in g st for 4 rows, ending with RS facing for next row.
Change to 4mm (US 6) needles.
Beg with a K row, work in st st for 2 [2: 2: 4: 4] rows, ending with RS facing for next row.
Next row (RS): K to last 14 sts, K2tog, K8, K2tog, K2.
Complete to match left front, reversing shapings.

SLEEVES

Using 3¼mm (US 3) needles cast on 26 [28: 28: 30: 30] sts.
Work in g st for 4 rows, ending with RS facing for next row.
Change to 4mm (US 6) needles.
Beg with a K row, work in st st, shaping sides by inc 1 st at each end of next [next: 3rd: 3rd: 3rd] and every foll alt [4th: 4th: 4th: 4th] row to 36 [46: 48: 46: 48] sts, then on every foll 4th [-: -: 6th: 6th] row until there are 44 [-: -: 50: 52] sts.
Cont straight until sleeve meas 12.5 [15: 17.5: 19.5: 21.5] cm, ending with RS facing for next row.
Shape raglan
Cast off 2 sts at beg of next 2 rows. 40 [42: 44: 46: 48] sts.
Working all raglan decreases as set by back raglan armholes, dec 1 st at each end of next and 2 foll 4th rows, then on every foll alt row until 20 sts rem.
Work 1 row, ending with RS facing for next row.
Left sleeve only
Dec 1 st at each end of next row, then cast off 4 sts at beg of foll row. 14 sts.
Dec 1 st at beg of next row, then cast off 4 sts at beg of foll row. 9 sts.
Right sleeve only
Cast off 5 sts at beg and dec 1 st at end of next row. 14 sts.
Work 1 row.
Cast off 4 sts at beg and dec 1 st at end of next row. 9 sts.
Work 1 row.

Both sleeves

Rep last 2 rows once more.
Cast off rem 4 sts.

MAKING UP

Press as described on the information page.
Join all raglan seams using back stitch, or mattress stitch if preferred.
Button band
With RS facing and using 3¼mm (US 3) needles, pick up and knit 48 [51: 54: 57: 60] sts evenly down left front opening edge, from neck shaping to cast-on edge.
Work in g st for 4 rows, ending with **WS** facing for next row.
Cast off knitwise (on **WS**).
Buttonhole band
With RS facing and using 3¼mm (US 3) needles, pick up and knit 48 [51: 54: 57: 60] sts evenly up right front opening edge, from cast-on edge to neck shaping.
Row 1 (WS): Knit.
Row 2: K31 [32: 33: 34: 35], *K2tog, yfwd (to make a buttonhole), K4 [5: 6: 7: 8], rep from * once more, K2tog, yfwd (to make 3rd buttonhole), K3.
Work in g st for a further 2 rows, ending with **WS** facing for next row.
Cast off knitwise (on **WS**).
Collar
Using 3¼mm (US 3) needles cast on 96 [100: 100: 104: 104] sts.
Work in g st for 3 rows, ending with **WS** facing for next row.
Next row (WS): Cast off 18 sts knitwise, P until there are 60 [64: 64: 68: 68] sts on right needle, cast off rem 18 sts knitwise. Break yarn.
Change to 4mm (US 6) needles.
With RS facing, rejoin yarn to centre 60 [64: 64: 68: 68] sts and K to end.
Beg with a P row, work in st st, inc 1 st at each end of next 3 rows. 66 [70: 70: 74: 74] sts.
Work a further 14 rows, ending with RS facing for next row.
Cast off 8 sts at beg of next 6 rows.
Cast off rem 18 [22: 22: 26: 26] sts.
Sew cast-off edge of first 4 rows to row-end edges of centre section, then sew shaped cast-off edge of collar to neck edge, positioning ends of collar halfway across top of bands.
See information page for finishing instructions.

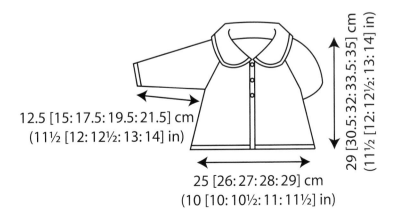

12.5 [15: 17.5: 19.5: 21.5] cm
(11½ [12: 12½: 13: 14] in)

29 [30.5: 32: 33.5: 35] cm
(11½ [12: 12½: 13: 14] in)

25 [26: 27: 28: 29] cm
(10 [10: 10½: 11: 11½] in)

YARN

To fit age

| 0-3 | 3-6 | 6-9 | 9-12 | 12-18 | | months |

Rowan Fine Milk Cotton

| 4 | 4 | 5 | 5 | 6 | | x 50gm |

(photographed in Pastille 494)

NEEDLES

1 pair 2mm (no 14) (US 0) needles
1 pair 2¾mm (no 12) (US 2) needles
2mm (no 14) (US 0) circular needle
Cable needle

BUTTONS

6 x BN1121 (natural) from Bedecked.
Please see information page for contact details.

TENSION

41 sts and 38 rows to 10 cm measured over patt using 2¾mm (US 2) needles.

SPECIAL ABBREVIATIONS

C4B = slip next 2 sts onto cable needle and leave at back of work, K2, then K2 from cable needle.

BACK

Using 2mm (US 0) needles cast on 104 [108: 112: 116: 120] sts.
Row 1 (RS): (K1, P1) 0 [0: 1: 0: 0] times, K2 [4: 4: 4: 2], *P1, K2, P1, K4, rep from * to last 6 [8: 2: 4: 6] sts, P1, K2 [2: 1: 2: 2], P1 [1: 0: 1: 1], K2 [4: 0: 0: 2].
Row 2: (P1, K1) 0 [0: 1: 0: 0] times, P2 [4: 4: 0: 2], *K1, P2, K1, P4, rep from * to last 6 [8: 2: 4: 6] sts, K1, P2 [2: 1: 2: 2], K1 [1: 0: 1: 1], P2 [4: 0: 0: 2].
Row 3: (K1, P1) 0 [0: 1: 0: 0] times, K2 [4: 0: 0: 2], (C4B) 0 [0: 1: 0: 0] times, *P1, K2, P1, C4B, rep from * to last 6 [8: 2: 4: 6] sts, P1, K2 [2: 1: 2: 2], P1 [1: 0: 1: 1], K2 [4: 0: 0: 2].
Row 4: As row 2.
These 4 rows form patt.
Change to 2¾mm (US 2) needles.
Cont in patt until back meas 14 [15: 16: 17: 18] cm, ending with RS facing for next row.
Shape armholes
Keeping patt correct, cast off 6 sts at beg of next 2 rows.
92 [96: 100: 104: 108] sts.
Dec 1 st at each end of next 6 rows, ending with RS facing for next row. 80 [84: 88: 92: 96] sts.
Work 34 [36: 38: 40: 42] rows, ending with RS facing for next row. (Armhole should meas 11 [11.5: 12: 12.5: 13] cm.)
Shape shoulders and back neck
Next row (RS): Cast off 7 [8: 9: 9: 10] sts, patt until there are 11 [11: 12: 13: 14] sts on right needle and turn, leaving rem sts on a holder.

Work each side of neck separately.
Cast off 3 sts at beg of next row.
Cast off rem 8 [8: 9: 10: 11] sts.
With RS facing, rejoin yarn to rem sts, cast off centre 44 [46: 46: 48: 48] sts, patt to end.
Complete to match first side, reversing shapings.

RIGHT FRONT

Using 2mm (US 0) needles cast on 77 [79: 81: 83: 85] sts.
Row 1 (RS): K2, P1, K4, *P1, K2, P1, K4, rep from * to last 6 [8: 2: 4: 6] sts, P1, K2 [2: 1: 2: 2], P1 [1: 0: 1: 1], K2 [4: 0: 0: 2].
Row 2: (P1, K1) 0 [0: 1: 0: 0] times, P2 [4: 4: 0: 2], *K1, P2, K1, P4, rep from * to last 3 sts, K1, P2.
Row 3: K2, P1, C4B, *P1, K2, P1, C4B, rep from * to last 6 [8: 2: 4: 6] sts, P1, K2 [2: 1: 2: 2], P1 [1: 0: 1: 1], K2 [4: 0: 0: 2].
Row 4: As row 2.
These 4 rows form patt.
Change to 2¾mm (US 2) needles.
Cont in patt until right front matches back to beg of armhole shaping, ending with RS facing for next row.
Shape armhole
Work 1 row.
Keeping patt correct, cast off 6 sts at beg of next row.
71 [73: 75: 77: 79] sts.
Dec 1 st at armhole edge of next 6 rows, ending with RS facing for next row. 65 [67: 69: 71: 73] sts.
Work 2 rows, ending with RS facing for next row.
Shape front slope
Keeping patt correct, dec 2 sts at beg of next row by casting off 2 sts.
Dec 2 sts at end of next row by working 3 sts tog.
Working all decreases as set by last 2 rows, dec 2 sts at front slope edge of next 19 [18: 16: 15: 13] rows.
23 [27: 33: 37: 43] sts.
Now dec 1 st at front slope edge of next 8 [11: 15: 18: 22] rows.

15 [16: 18: 19: 21] sts.
Work 3 rows, ending with RS facing for next row.
Shape shoulder
Cast off 7 [8: 9: 9: 10] sts at beg of next row.
Work 1 row.
Cast off rem 8 [8: 9: 10: 11] sts.
Mark positions for 3 pairs of buttons along right front opening edge − first pair in row 13, top pair 2 rows below beg of front slope shaping, and rem pair evenly spaced between.

LEFT FRONT

Using 2mm (US 0) needles cast on 77 [79: 81: 83: 85] sts.
Row 1 (RS): (K1, P1) 0 [0: 1: 0: 0] times, K2 [4: 4: 0: 2], ★P1, K2, P1, K4, rep from ★ to last 3 sts, P1, K2.
Row 2: P2, K1, P4, ★K1, P2, K1, P4, rep from ★ to last 6 [8: 2: 4: 6] sts, K1, P2 [2: 1: 2: 2], K1 [1: 0: 1: 1], P2 [4: 0: 0: 2].
Row 3: (K1, P1) 0 [0: 1: 0: 0] times, K2 [4: 0: 0: 2], (C4B) 0 [0: 1: 0: 0] times, ★P1, K2, P1, C4B, rep from ★ to last 3 sts, P1, K2.
Row 4: As row 2.
These 4 rows form patt.
Change to 2¾mm (US 2) needles.
Cont in patt for a further 8 rows, ending with RS facing for next row.
Row 13 (buttonhole row) (RS): Patt to last 31 [33: 35: 37: 39] sts, cast off 2 sts (to make first buttonhole of first pair − cast on 2 sts over these cast-off sts on next row), patt to last 6 sts, cast off 2 sts (to make 2nd buttonhole of first pair − cast on 2 sts over these cast-off sts on next row), patt to end.
Making a further 2 pairs of buttonholes in this way to correspond with positions marked for buttons on right front, complete to match right front, reversing shapings.

SLEEVES

Using 2mm (US 0) needles cast on 54 [58: 58: 62: 62] sts.
Row 1 (RS): P0 [0: 0: 1: 1], K1 [3: 3: 4: 4], ★P1, K2, P1, K4, rep from ★ to last 5 [7: 7: 1: 1] sts, P1, (K2, P1) 1 [1: 1: 0: 0] times, K1 [3: 3: 0: 0].

Row 2: K0 [0: 0: 1: 1], P1 [3: 3: 4: 4], ★K1, P2, K1, P4, rep from ★ to last 5 [7: 7: 1: 1] sts, K1, (P2, K1) 1 [1: 1: 0: 0] times, P1 [3: 3: 0: 0].
Row 3: P0 [0: 0: 1: 1], K1 [3: 3: 0: 0], (C4B) 0 [0: 0: 1: 1] times, ★P1, K2, P1, C4B, rep from ★ to last 5 [7: 7: 1: 1] sts, P1, (K2, P1) 1 [1: 1: 0: 0] times, K1 [3: 3: 0: 0].
Row 4: As row 2.
These 4 rows form patt.
Change to 2¾mm (US 2) needles.
Cont in patt, shaping sides by inc 1 st at each end of next and every foll alt row to 88 [82: 84: 82: 82] sts, then on every foll 4th row until there are 90 [94: 98: 102: 106] sts, taking inc sts into patt.
Cont straight until sleeve meas 12.5 [15: 17.5: 19.5: 21.5] cm, ending with RS facing for next row.
Shape top
Keeping patt correct, cast off 6 sts at beg of next 2 rows.
78 [82: 86: 90: 94] sts.
Dec 1 st at each end of next and foll 4 alt rows, then on foll row, ending with RS facing for next row.
Cast off rem 66 [70: 74: 78: 82] sts.

MAKING UP

Press as described on the information page.
Join both shoulder seams using back stitch, or mattress stitch if preferred.
Front band
With RS facing and using 2mm (US 0) circular needle, beg and ending at cast-on edges, pick up and knit 52 [55: 58: 61: 64] sts up right front opening edge to beg of front slope shaping, 48 [50: 52: 54: 56] sts up right front slope, 40 [42: 42: 44: 44] sts from back, 48 [50: 52: 54: 56] sts down left front slope to beg of front slope shaping, then 52 [55: 58: 61: 64] sts down left front opening edge. 240 [252: 262: 274: 284] sts.
Work in g st for 4 rows, ending with **WS** facing for next row.
Cast off knitwise (on **WS**).
See information page for finishing instructions, setting in sleeves using the shallow set-in method.

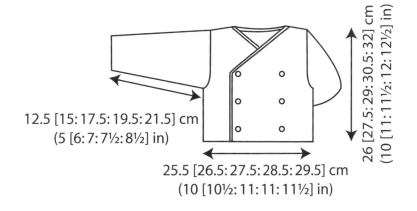

12.5 [15: 17.5: 19.5: 21.5] cm
(5 [6: 7: 7½: 8½] in)

25.5 [26.5: 27.5: 28.5: 29.5] cm
(10 [10½: 11: 11: 11½] in)

26 [27.5: 29: 30.5: 32] cm
(10 [11: 11½: 12: 12½] in)

sunshine

Designer: Martin Storey

main image page 30, 31 & 32

To fit age

0-3	3-6	6-9	9-12	12-18			
					2	3	years

months / years

| 2 | 3 | 3 | 3 | 3 | 4 | 4 | x 50gm |

(photographed in Cloud 497 and Kiwi 485)

1 pair 4mm (no 8) (US 6) needles
1 pair 5mm (no 6) (US 8) needles

6-9 month version; 1 x BN1150 (small), 1 x BN1121 (natural), 1 x RW5022. 12-18 month version; 1 x BN1150 (small), 1 x BN1121, 1 x BN1132.
All buttons from Bedecked.
Please see information page for contact details.

21 sts and 30 rows to 10 cm measured over st st using 5mm (US 8) needles.

BACK

Using 4mm (US 6) needles cast on 53 [55: 57: 59: 61: 63: 65] sts.
Row 1 (RS): Purl.
Row 2: Knit.
Row 3: K1 [2: 3: 1: 2: 3: 1], P3, *K3, P3, rep from * to last 1 [2: 3: 1: 2: 3: 1] sts, K1 [2: 3: 1: 2: 3: 1].
Row 4: P1 [2: 3: 1: 2: 3: 1], K3, *P3, K3, rep from * to last 1 [2: 3: 1: 2: 3: 1] sts, P1 [2: 3: 1: 2: 3: 1].
Rows 5 to 14: As rows 3 and 4, 5 times.
Change to 5mm (US 8) needles.
Beg with a K row, work in st st until back meas 13.5 [14.5: 15.5: 16: 17: 18: 18.5] cm, ending with RS facing for next row.
Shape raglan armholes
Cast off 2 sts at beg of next 2 rows.
49 [51: 53: 55: 57: 59: 61] sts.★★
Next row (RS): K2, sl 1, K1, psso, K to last 4 sts, K2tog, K2.
Next row: K2, P to last 2 sts, K2.
Next row: Knit.
Next row: K2, P to last 2 sts, K2.
Rep last 4 rows 1 [1: 1: 2: 2: 3: 3] times more. 45 [47: 49: 49: 51: 51: 53] sts.
Next row (RS): K2, sl 1, K1, psso, K to last 4 sts, K2tog, K2.
Next row: K2, P to last 2 sts, K2.
Rep last 2 rows 11 [12: 13: 12: 13: 12: 13] times more, ending with RS facing for next row.
Cast off rem 21 [21: 21: 23: 23: 25: 25] sts.

Work as given for back to ★★.
Working all raglan armhole decreases as set by back raglan armholes, work 0 [2: 4: 6: 6: 8: 10] rows, dec 1 st at each end of

– [next: next: next: next: next: next] and – [0: 0: 1: 1: 1: 2] foll 4th rows and ending with RS facing for next row.
49 [49: 51: 51: 53: 55: 55] sts.
Divide for front opening
Next row (RS): (K2, sl 1, K1, psso) 1 [0: 1: 0: 0: 1: 0] times, K18 [22: 19: 23: 24: 21: 25] and turn, leaving rem sts on a holder. 21 [22: 22: 23: 24: 24: 25] sts.
Work each side of neck separately.
Dec 1 st at raglan armhole edge of 4th [2nd: 4th: 2nd: 2nd: 4th: 2nd] and 1 [1: 0: 1: 1: 1: 1] foll 4th row, then on foll 5 [6: 7: 6: 6: 5: 6] alt rows, ending with **WS** facing for next row.
14 [14: 14: 15: 16: 17: 17] sts.
Shape neck
Cast off 4 [4: 4: 5: 4: 5: 5] sts at beg of next row.
10 [10: 10: 10: 12: 12: 12] sts.
Dec 1 st at neck edge of next 4 [4: 4: 4: 5: 5: 5] rows **and at same time** dec 1 st at raglan armhole edge of next and foll 1 [1: 1: 1: 2: 2: 2] alt rows. 4 sts.
Work 0 [0: 0: 0: 1: 1: 1] row, ending with RS facing for next row.
Next row (RS): K1, sl 1, K2tog, psso.
Next row: K2.
Next row: K2tog and fasten off.
With RS facing, rejoin yarn to rem sts, cast off centre 5 sts, K to last 4 [0: 4: 0: 0: 4: 0] sts, (K2tog, K2) 1 [0: 1: 0: 0: 1: 0] times.
21 [22: 22: 23: 24: 24: 25] sts.
Complete to match first side, reversing shapings.

Using 4mm (US 6) needles cast on 27 [29: 29: 31: 31: 33: 33] sts.
Row 1 (RS): Purl.
Row 2: Knit.
Row 3: K0 [1: 1: 2: 2: 3: 3], P3, *K3, P3, rep from * to last 0 [1: 1: 2: 2: 3: 3] sts, K0 [1: 1: 2: 2: 3: 3].
Row 4: P0 [1: 1: 2: 2: 3: 3], K3, *P3, K3, rep from * to last 0 [1:

1: 2: 2: 3: 3] sts, P0 [1: 1: 2: 2: 3: 3].

Rows 5 to 8: As rows 3 and 4, twice.

Change to 5mm (US 8) needles.

Beg with a K row, work in st st, shaping sides by inc 1 st at each end of next [next: next: next: next: 3rd: 3rd] and every foll alt [alt: alt: alt: 4th: 4th: 4th] row to 45 [39: 35: 35: 55: 51: 49] sts, then on every foll 4th [4th: 4th: 4th: -: 6th: 6th] row until there are 47 [49: 51: 53: -: 57: 59] sts.

Cont straight until sleeve meas 12 [14.5: 17: 19: 21: 23.5: 26] cm, ending with RS facing for next row.

Shape raglan

Cast off 2 sts at beg of next 2 rows.

43 [45: 47: 49: 51: 53: 55] sts.

Working all raglan decreases as set by back raglan armholes, dec 1 st at each end of next and 2 foll 4th rows, then on every foll alt row until 21 sts rem.

Work 1 row, ending with RS facing for next row.

Left sleeve only

Dec 1 st at each end of next row, then cast off 4 sts at beg of foll row. 15 sts.

Dec 1 st at beg of next row, then cast off 4 sts at beg of foll row. 10 sts.

Right sleeve only

Cast off 5 sts at beg and dec 1 st at end of next row. 15 sts.

Work 1 row.

Cast off 4 sts at beg and dec 1 st at end of next row. 10 sts.

Work 1 row.

Both sleeves

Rep last 2 rows once more.

Cast off rem 5 sts.

Press as described on the information page.

Join all raglan seams using back stitch, or mattress stitch

if preferred.

Neckband

With RS facing and using 4mm (US 6) needles, beg and ending at front opening edges, pick up and knit 8 [8: 8: 10: 10: 10: 10] sts up right side of neck, 16 sts from top of right sleeve, 21 [21: 21: 23: 23: 23: 23] sts from back, 16 sts from top of left sleeve, then 8 [8: 8: 10: 10: 10: 10] sts down left side of neck. 69 [69: 69: 75: 75: 75: 75] sts.

Row 1 (WS): P3, ★K3, P3, rep from ★ to end.

Row 2: K3, ★P3, K3, rep from ★ to end.

These 2 rows form rib.

Cont in rib until neckband meas 3 cm, ending with RS facing for next row.

Cast off in rib.

Button band

Using 4mm (US 6) needles cast on 6 sts.

Work in g st until band, when slightly stretched, fits up front opening edge (left front for a girl or right front for a boy) from cast-off sts at base of front opening to top of neckband, ending with RS facing for next row.

Cast off.

Slip stitch band in place. Mark positions for 3 buttons on this band – first button to come 1.5 cm up from base of front opening, top button to come 1.5 cm down from top of neckband and rem button evenly spaced between.

Buttonhole band

Work to match button band, with the addition of 3 buttonholes worked to correspond with positions marked for buttons as folls:

Buttonhole row (RS): K2, cast off 2 sts (to make a buttonhole – cast on 2 sts over these cast-off sts on next row), K to end.

Slip stitch this band in place. Lay buttonhole band over button band and sew cast-on edges to cast-off sts at base of opening.

See information page for finishing instructions.

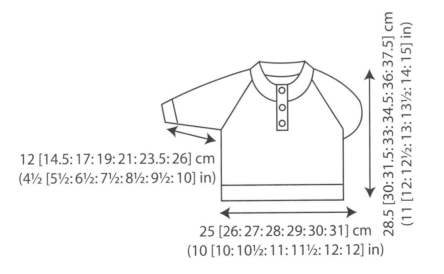

12 [14.5: 17: 19: 21: 23.5: 26] cm
(4½ [5½: 6½: 7½: 8½: 9½: 10] in)

28.5 [30: 31.5: 33: 34.5: 36: 37.5] cm
(11 [12: 12½: 13: 13½: 14: 15] in)

25 [26: 27: 28: 29: 30: 31] cm
(10 [10: 10½: 11: 11½: 12: 12] in)

Designer: Martin Storey

main image page 14 & 15

YARN

To fit age		12-18			months
			2	3	years
Rowan Fine Milk Cotton					
A	Humbugs 484	2	2	2	x 50gm
B	Lagoon 504	1	1	1	x 50gm
C	Snow 493	1	1	1	x 50gm

NEEDLES

1 pair 2mm (no 14) (US 0) needles
1 pair 2¾mm (no 12) (US 2) needles

BUTTONS

3 x BN1366 from Bedecked.
Please see information page for contact details.

TENSION

30 sts and 38 rows to 10 cm measured over patterned st st using 2¾mm (US 2) needles.

BACK

Using 2mm (US 0) needles and yarn B cast on 85 [87: 91] sts.
Row 1 (RS): K2 [3: 0], P3 [3: 2], ★K3, P3, rep from ★ to last 2 [3: 5] sts, K2 [3: 3], P0 [0: 2].
Row 2: P2 [3: 0], K3 [3: 2], ★P3, K3, rep from ★ to last 2 [3: 5] sts, P2 [3: 3], K0 [0: 2].
These 2 rows form rib.
Keeping rib correct, now work in stripes as folls:
Rows 3 to 6: Using yarn A.
Rows 7 and 8: Using yarn B.
Rows 9 to 20: As rows 3 to 8, twice.
Rows 21 and 22: Using yarn A.
These 22 rows complete striped rib.
Change to 2¾mm (US 2) needles.★★
Beg and ending rows as indicated, using the **fairisle** technique as described on the information page, now work in patt from chart, which is worked entirely in st st beg with a K row, as folls:
Work chart rows 1 to 6, ending with RS facing for next row.
Break off contrasts and cont using yarn A only.
Work in st st for 36 [40: 44] rows, ending with RS facing for next row. (Back should meas 17 [18: 19] cm.)
Shape armholes
Cast off 6 sts at beg of next 2 rows. 73 [75: 79] sts.
Dec 1 st at each end of next 3 rows, then on foll 3 [3: 4] alt rows, then on foll 4th row. 59 [61: 63] sts.
Work 9 [11: 13] rows, ending with RS facing for next row.
Divide for back opening
Next row (RS): K28 [29: 30] and turn, leaving rem sts on a holder.
Work each side of neck separately.
Work 25 rows, ending with RS facing for next row.

(Armhole should meas 13 [13.5: 14.5] cm.)
Shape shoulder and back neck
Next row (RS): Cast off 5 sts, K until there are 8 [8: 9] sts on right needle and turn, leaving rem 15 [16: 16] sts on a second holder.
Cast off 3 sts at beg of next row.
Cast off rem 5 [5: 6] sts.
With RS facing, rejoin yarn to rem sts on first holder, cast off centre 3 sts, K to end.
Complete to match first side, reversing shapings.

FRONT

Work as given for back to ★★.
Beg and ending rows as indicated, using the **fairisle** technique for chart rows 3 to 6 and the **intarsia** technique for all other rows as described on the information page, now work in patt from chart, which is worked entirely in st st beg with a K row, as folls:
Work 42 [46: 50] rows, ending with RS facing for next row.
Shape armholes
Keeping patt correct, cast off 6 sts at beg of next 2 rows.
73 [75: 79] sts.
Dec 1 st at each end of next 3 rows, then on foll 3 [3: 4] alt rows, then on foll 4th row.
59 [61: 63] sts.
Cont straight until chart row 76 [82: 90] has been completed, ending with RS facing for next row.
Shape front neck
Next row (RS): Patt 18 [18: 19] sts and turn, leaving rem sts on a holder.
Work each side of neck separately.
Keeping patt correct, dec 1 st at neck edge of next 4 rows, then on foll 3 alt rows, then on foll 4th row. 10 [10: 11] sts.
Work 1 row, ending after chart row 92 [98: 106] and with RS facing for next row.

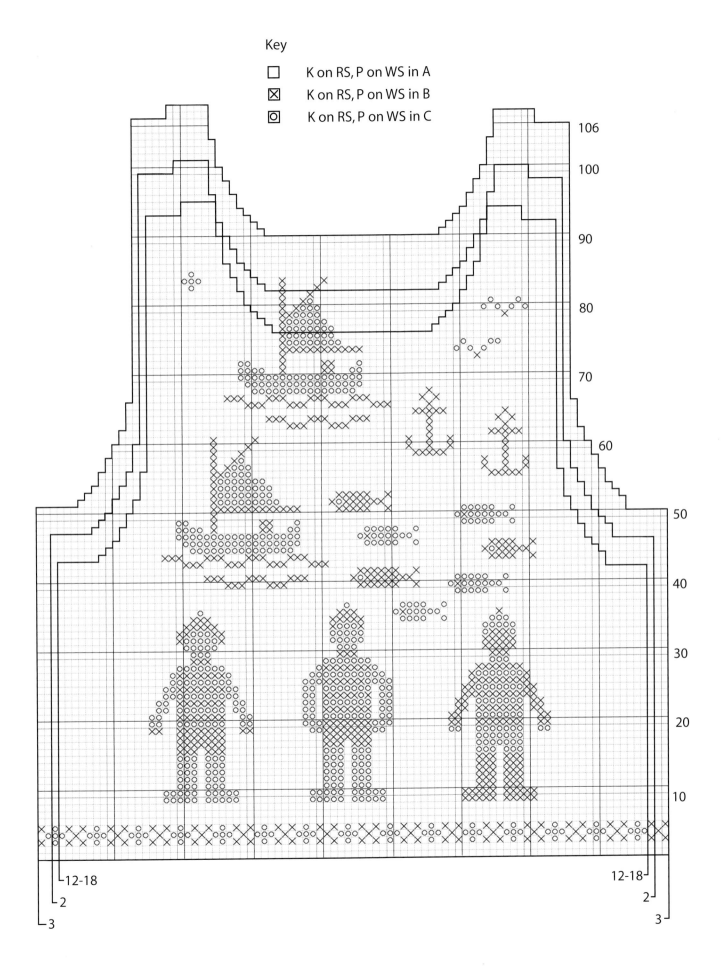

Key

☐   K on RS, P on WS in A

☒   K on RS, P on WS in B

⊙   K on RS, P on WS in C

106

100

90

80

70

60

50

40

30

20

10

12-18

2

3

12-18

2

3

Shape shoulder

Cast off 5 sts at beg of next row.

Work 1 row.

Cast off rem 5 [5: 6] sts.

With RS facing, slip centre 23 [25: 25] sts onto a holder, rejoin yarn to rem sts, patt to end.

Complete to match first side, reversing shapings.

MAKING UP

Press as described on the information page.

Join both shoulder seams using back stitch, or mattress stitch if preferred.

Buttonhole border

With RS facing, using 2mm (US 0) needles and yarn B, pick up and knit 21 sts evenly up left side of back opening, from cast-off sts at base of opening to sts left on holder at neck edge.

Work in g st for 3 rows, ending with RS facing for next row.

Row 4 (RS): K5, (K2tog, yfwd, K6) twice.

Work in g st for a further 2 rows, ending with **WS** facing for next row.

Cast off knitwise (on **WS**).

Lay buttonhole band over button band and sew row-end edges of bands to cast-off sts at base of opening.

Button border

With RS facing, using 2mm (US 0) needles and yarn B, pick up and knit 21 sts evenly down right side of back opening, from sts left on holder at neck edge to cast-off sts at base of opening.

Work in g st for 6 rows, ending with **WS** facing for next row.

Cast off knitwise (on **WS**).

Neckband

With RS facing, using 2mm (US 0) needles and yarn B, pick up and knit 5 sts across top of buttonhole band, K15 [16: 16] sts on left back holder, pick up and knit 5 sts up left side of back neck and 16 sts down left side of front neck, K23 [25: 25] sts on front holder, pick up and knit 16 sts up right side of front neck and 5 sts down right side of back neck, K15 [16: 16] sts on right back holder, then pick up and knit 5 sts across top of button band. 105 [109: 109] sts.

Work in g st for 3 rows, ending with RS facing for next row.

Row 4 (RS): K2, K2tog, yfwd, K to end.

Work in g st for a further 2 rows, ending with **WS** facing for next row.

Cast off knitwise (on **WS**).

Armhole borders (both alike)

With RS facing, using 2mm (US 0) needles and yarn B, pick up and knit 103 [103: 109] sts evenly all round armhole edge.

Row 1 (WS): P2, ★K3, P3, rep from ★ to last 5 sts, K3, P2.

Row 2: K2, ★P3, K3, rep from ★ to last 5 sts, P3, K2.

These 2 rows form rib.

Join in yarn A.

Using yarn A, work in rib for a further 2 rows.

Break off yarn A.

Using yarn B, work in rib for a further 2 rows, ending with **WS** facing for next row.

Cast off in rib (on **WS**).

See information page for finishing instructions.

31 [33: 35] cm
(12 [13: 14] in)

28.5 [29: 30.5] cm
(11 [11½: 12] in)

patch blanket

Designer: Martin Storey

main image page 9

YARN

Rowan Cashsoft DK

A	Blink 534	12	x 50gm
B	Lichen 523	2	x 50gm
C	Clementine 510	2	x 50gm
D	Blue Jacket 535	2	x 50gm
E	Lime 509	2	x 50gm
F	Bloom 520	2	x 50gm
G	Mirage 503	2	x 50gm
H	Poppy 512	2	x 50gm
J	Mist 505	2	x 50gm

NEEDLES

1 pair 3³/₄mm (no 9) (US 5) needles

TENSION

22½ sts and 40 rows to 10 cm measured over g st using 3³/₄mm (US 5) needles. Each patch measures 12 cm square.

FINISHED SIZE

Completed blanket measures approx 115 cm (45½ ins) square.

PATCH (make 85)

Using 3³/₄mm (US 5) needles and yarn A cast on 27 sts.
Work in g st for 49 rows, ending with **WS** facing for next row.
Cast off knitwise (on **WS**).
Now make a further 84 patches in colours as folls: a further 48 patches using yarn A, 5 patches using each of yarns B, D, F and H, and 4 patches using each of yarns C, E, G and J.

MAKING UP

Press as described on the information page.
Following diagram, join patches to form one large square 7 patches wide and 7 patches long, alternating direction of knitting in a checkerboard fashion as indicated by arrows at top right of diagram. Using colours at random and photograph as a guide, work in blanket stitch around entire outer edge of blanket.

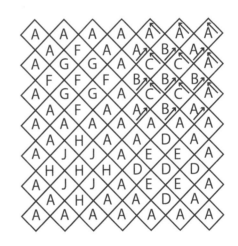

sizing guide

When you knit a Rowan baby or children's design, we want you to be happy with the look and feel of the finished garment. This all starts with the size and fit of the design you choose. To help you to achieve the correct fit for your baby or child, we have looked at the sizing of our baby and children's patterns. This has resulted in the introduction of the sizing chart below.

Dimensions in the chart below are body measurements, not garment dimensions, therefore please refer to the measuring guide to help you to determine which is the best size for your baby or child.

MEASURING GUIDE

For maximum comfort and to ensure the correct fit when choosing the size to knit, please follow the tips below when checking the size of your baby or child.

Measure your baby or child gently, close to the body over their underwear, but don't pull the tape measure too tight!

- **Height** – measure from the top of your baby's or child head to their feet when they are laying or standing straight.

- **Chest** – measure around the fullest part of the chest and across the shoulder blades.

- **Waist** – measure around the natural waistline just above the hip bone.

- **Hips** – measure around the fullest part of the bottom.

If you don't wish to measure your baby or child, note the size of their or your favourite jumper that you like the fit of. Our sizes are comparable to the clothing sizes from the major high street retailers, so if the favourite jumper is 6 months or 3 years, then our 6 months or 3 years size should measure approximately the same. Measure this favourite jumper and compare the measurements against the size diagram at the end of the pattern you wish to knit.

Finally, once you have decided which size is best for you to knit, please ensure that you achieve the correct tension for the design you are planning to knit.

Remember if your tension is too loose, your garment will be bigger than the pattern size and you may use more yarn. If your tension is too tight, your garment will be smaller than the pattern size and you may have yarn left over. Furthermore if your tension is incorrect, the handle of your fabric will be either too stiff or too floppy and will not fit properly. As you invest money and time in knitting one of our designs, it really does make sense to check your tension before starting your project.

STANDARD SIZING GUIDE FOR BABIES & CHILDREN

AGE	0-3 m	3-6 m	6-9 m	9-12 m	12-18 m	2 yr	3 yr	
To fit height	22 - 24.5	24.5 - 26.5	26.5 - 29	29 - 31.5	31.5 - 34	36	98	inches
	56 - 62	62 - 68	68 - 74	74 - 80	80 - 86	92	38.5	cm
Weight	10 - 14	14 - 18	18 - 21	21 - 24				lbs
	4.5 - 6	6 - 8	8 - 9.5	9.5 - 11				kgs
To fit chest					19.25 - 20	20.75	55	inches
					49 - 51	53	21.75	cm
To fit waist					19.5 - 20	20.5	53	inches
					50 - 51	52	20.75	cm
To fit hips					20.5 - 21.25	22	58	inches
					52 - 54	56	22.75	cm

information

Tension

Obtaining the correct tension is perhaps the single factor which can make the difference between a successful garment and a disastrous one. It controls both the shape and size of an article, so any variation, however slight, can distort the finished garment. Different designers feature in our books and it is their tension, given at the start of each pattern, which you must match. We recommend that you knit a square in pattern and/or stocking stitch (depending on the pattern instructions) of perhaps 5 - 10 more stitches and 5 - 10 more rows than those given in the tension note. Mark out the central 10cm square with pins. If you have too many stitches to 10cm try again using thicker needles, if you have too few stitches to 10cm try again using finer needles. Once you have achieved the correct tension your garment will be knitted to the measurements indicated in the size diagram shown at the end of the pattern.

Sizing and Size Diagram Note

The instructions are given for the smallest size. Where they vary, work the figures in brackets for the larger sizes. One set of figures refers to all sizes. Included with most patterns in this magazine is a 'size diagram', or sketch of the finished garment and its dimensions. The size diagram shows the finished width of the garment at the under-arm point, and it is this measurement that the knitter should choose first; a useful tip is to measure one of your own garments which is a comfortable fit. Having chosen a size based on width, look at the corresponding length for that size; if you are not happy with the total length which we recommend, adjust your own garment before beginning your armhole shaping - any adjustment after this point will mean that your sleeve will not fit into your garment easily - don't forget to take your adjustment into account if there is any side seam shaping. Finally, look at the sleeve length; the size diagram shows the finished sleeve measurement, taking into account any top-arm insertion length. Measure your body between the centre of your neck and your wrist, this measurement should correspond to half the garment width plus the sleeve length. Again, your sleeve length may be adjusted, but remember to take into consideration your sleeve increases if you do adjust the length - you must increase more frequently than the pattern states to shorten your sleeve, less frequently to lengthen it.

Chart Note

Many of the patterns in the book are worked from charts. Each square on a chart represents a stitch and each line of squares a row of knitting. Each colour used is given a different letter and these are shown in the materials section, or in the key alongside the chart of each pattern. When working from the charts, read odd rows (K) from right to left and even rows (P) from left to right, unless otherwise stated.

Knitting with colour

There are two main methods of working colour into a knitted fabric: Intarsia and Fairisle techniques. The first method produces a single thickness of fabric and is usually used where a colour is only required in a particular area of a row and does not form a repeating pattern across the row, as in the fairisle technique.
Intarsia: The simplest way to do this is to cut short lengths of yarn for each motif or block of colour used in a row. Then joining in the various colours at the appropriate point on the row, link one colour to the next by twisting them around each other where they meet on the wrong side to avoid gaps. All ends can then either be darned along the colour join lines, as each motif is completed or then can be "knitted-in" to the fabric of the knitting as each colour is worked into the pattern. This is done in much the same way as "weaving-in" yarns when working the Fairisle technique and does save time darning-in ends. It is essential that the tension is noted for Intarsia as this may vary from the stocking stitch if both are used in the same pattern.
Fairisle type knitting: When two or three colours are worked repeatedly across a row, strand the yarn not in use loosely behind the stitches being worked. If you are working with more than two colours, treat the "floating" yarns as if they were one yarn and always spread the stitches to their correct width to keep them elastic. It is advisable not to carry the stranded or "floating" yarns over more than three stitches at a time, but to weave them under and over the colour you are working. The "floating" yarns are caught at the back of the work.

Finishing Instructions

After working for hours knitting a garment, it seems a great pity that many garments are spoiled because such little care is taken in the pressing and finishing process. Follow the following tips for a truly professional-looking garment.

Pressing

Block out each piece of knitting and following the instructions on the ball band press the garment pieces, omitting the ribs. Tip: Take special care to press the edges, as this will make sewing up both easier and neater. If the ball band indicates that the fabric is not to be pressed, then covering the blocked out fabric with a damp white cotton cloth and leaving it to stand will have the desired effect. Darn in all ends neatly along the selvedge edge or a colour join, as appropriate.

Stitching

When stitching the pieces together, remember to match areas of colour and texture very carefully where they meet. Use a seam stitch such as back stitch or mattress stitch for all main knitting seams and join all ribs and neckband with mattress stitch, unless otherwise stated.

Construction

Having completed the pattern instructions, join left shoulder and neckband seams as detailed above. Sew the top of the sleeve to the body of the garment using the method detailed in the pattern, referring to the appropriate guide:

Set-in sleeves: Place centre of cast-off edge of sleeve to shoulder seam. Set in sleeve, easing sleeve head into armhole.

Straight cast-off sleeves: Place centre of cast-off edge of sleeve to shoulder seam. Sew top of sleeve to body.

Join side and sleeve seams. Slip stitch pocket edgings and linings into place. Sew on buttons to correspond with buttonholes. Ribbed welts and neckbands and any area of garter stitch should not be pressed.

Abbreviations

K	knit
P	purl
st(s)	stitch(es)
inc	increas(e)(ing)
dec	decreas(e)(ing)
st st	stocking stitch (1 row K, 1 row P)
g st	garter stitch (K every row)
beg	begin(ning)
foll	following
rem	remain(ing)
rep	repeat
alt	alternate
cont	continue
patt	pattern
tog	together
mm	millimetres
cm	centimetres
in(s)	inch(es)
RS	right side
WS	wrong side
sl 1	slip one stitch
sl 2	slip two stitches
psso	pass slipped stitch over
tbl	through back of loop
M1	make one stitch by picking up horizontal loop before next stitch and working into back of it
yrn	yarn round needle
yfwd	yarn forward
yon	yarn over needle
yfrn	yarn forward and round needle
meas	measures
0	no stitches, times, or rows
-	no stitches, times or rows for that size
approx	approximately
rev	reverse

Crochet Terms

UK crochet terms and abbreviations have been used throughout. The list below gives the US equivalent where they vary.

Abbrev.	UK	US
dc	double crochet	single crochet
htr	half treble	half double crochet
tr	treble	double crochet
dtr	double treble	treble

= Easy, straight forward knitting/crocheting

= Suitable for the average knitter

= For the more experienced knitter

stockists

AUSTRALIA: Australian Country Spinners, Pty Ltd, Level 7, 409 St. Kilda Road, Melbourne Vic 3004. Tel: 03 9380 3830 Fax: 03 9820 0989
Email: sales@auspinners.com.au

AUSTRIA: Coats Harlander GmbH, Autokaderstrasse 31,
A -1210 Wien. Tel: (01) 27716 – 0
Fax: (01) 27716 - 228

BELGIUM: Coats Benelux, Ring Oost 14A, Ninove, 9400, Belgium
Tel: 0346 35 37 00 Email:
sales.coatsninove@coats.com

CANADA: Westminster Fibers Inc, 165 Ledge St, Nashua, NH03060
Tel: (1 603) 886 5041 / 5043
Fax: (1 603) 886 1056
Email: rowan@westminsterfibers.com

CHINA: Coats Shanghai Ltd, No 9 Building , Baosheng Road, Songjiang Industrial Zone, Shanghai. Tel: (86- 21) 5774 3733   Fax: (86-21) 5774 3768

DENMARK: Coats Danmark A/S, Nannasgade 28, 2200 Kobenhavn N
Tel: (45) 35 86 90 50
Fax: (45) 35 82 15 10
Email: info@hpgruppen.dk Web:
www.hpgruppen.dk

FINLAND: Coats Opti Oy, Ketjutie 3, 04220 Kerava Tel: (358) 9 274 871
Fax: (358) 9 2748 7330
Email: coatsopti.sales@coats.com

FRANCE: Coats France / Steiner Frères, SAS 100, avenue du Général de Gaulle, 18 500 Mehun-Sur-Yèvre
Tel: (33) 02 48 23 12 30
Fax: (33) 02 48 23 12 40

GERMANY: Coats GmbH, Kaiserstrasse 1, D-79341 Kenzingen
Tel: (49) 7644 8020 Fax: (49) 7644 802399 Web: www.coatsgmbh.de

HOLLAND: Coats Benelux, Ring Oost 14A, Ninove, 9400, Belgium
Tel: 0346 35 37 00 Email:
sales.coatsninove@coats.com

HONG KONG: Coats China Holdings Ltd, 19/F Millennium City 2, 378 Kwun Tong Road, Kwun Tong, Kowloon Tel: (852) 2798 6886 Fax: (852) 2305 0311

ICELAND: Storkurinn, Laugavegi 59, 101 Reykjavik Tel: (354) 551 8258 Email: storkurinn@simnet.is

ITALY: Coats Cucirini s.r.l., Via Sarca 223, 20126 Milano
Tel: 800 992377   Fax: 0266111701 Email: servizio.clienti@coats.com

KOREA: Coats Korea Co Ltd, 5F Kuckdong B/D, 935-40 Bangbae- Dong, Seocho-Gu, Seoul Tel: (82) 2 521 6262. Fax: (82) 2 521 5181

LEBANON: y.knot, Saifi Village, Mkhalissiya Street 162, Beirut
Tel: (961) 1 992211   Fax: (961) 1 315553
Email: y.knot@cyberia.net.lb

LUXEMBOURG: Coats Benelux, Ring Oost 14A, Ninove, 9400, Belgium
Tel: 054 318989 Email:
sales.coatsninove@coats.com

MALTA: John Gregory Ltd, 8 Ta'Xbiex Sea Front, Msida MSD 1512, Malta
Tel: +356 2133 0202, Fax: +356 2134 4745, e-mail: raygreg@onvol.net

MEXICO: Estambres Crochet SA de CV, Aaron Saenz
1891-7, Monterrey, NL 64650 Mexico
Tel: +52 (81) 8335-3870

NEW ZEALAND: ACS New Zealand, 1 March Place, Belfast, Christchurch
Tel: 64-3-323-6665 Fax: 64-3-323-6660

NORWAY: Coats Knappehuset AS, Pb 100 Ulset, 5873 Bergen
Tel: (47) 55 53 93 00
Fax: (47) 55 53 93 93

SINGAPORE: Golden Dragon Store, 101 Upper Cross Street #02-51, People's Park Centre, Singapore 058357
Tel: (65) 6 5358454   Fax: (65) 6 2216278
Email: gdscraft@hotmail.com

SOUTH AFRICA: Arthur Bales LTD, 62 4th Avenue, Linden 2195
Tel: (27) 11 888 2401
Fax: (27) 11 782 6137
Email: arthurb@new.co.za

SPAIN: Coats Fabra, Santa Adria 20, 08030 Barcelona
Tel: 932908400   Fax: 932908409
Email: atencion.clientes@coats.com

SWEDEN: Coats Expotex AB, Division Craft, Box 297, 401 24 Goteborg
Tel: (46) 33 720 79 00
Fax: 46 31 47 16 50

SWITZERLAND: Coats Stroppel AG, Stroppelstr.16 CH -5300 Turgi (AG)
Tel: (41) 562981220
Fax: (41) 56 298 12 50

TAIWAN: Cactus Quality Co Ltd, P.O.Box 30 485, Taipei, Taiwan, R.O.C., Office: 7FL-2, No 140, Roosevelt Road, Sec 2,Taipei, Taiwan, R.O.C.
Tel: 886-2-23656527
Fax: 886-2-23656503
Email: cqcl@m17.hinet.net

THAILAND: Global Wide Trading, 10 Lad Prao Soi 88, Bangkok 10310
Tel: 00 662 933 9019
Fax: 00 662 933 9110
Email: global.wide@yahoo.com

U.S.A.: Westminster Fibers Inc, 165 Ledge St, Nashua, NH03060
Tel: (1 603) 886 5041 / 5043
Fax: (1 603) 886 1056
Email: rowan@westminsterfibers.com

U.K: Rowan, Green Lane Mill, Holmfirth, West Yorkshire, England HD9 2DX
Tel: +44 (0) 1484 681881
Fax: +44 (0) 1484 687920
Email: mail@knitrowan.com Web:
www.knitrowan.com

For stockists in all other countries please contact Rowan for details